DECODI

GW00858522

DIEGO G_____

DECODING CHINA
Cross-cultural strategies for successful
business with the Chinese

Copyright © 2017 itim International
All rights reserved.
ISBN: 1537526502
ISBN-13: 978-1537526508

First published in 2017 by itim International

Published by itim International
Arabiankatu 12
FIN-00560 Helsinki
Finland
www.itim.org

©Editorial matter and selection itim International Oy
Author Diego Gilardoni
First edition 2017

Editor (language): Robert Brooks
Cover design and layout: Celia Zanin-Lassila
Cover photograph: Dave Tang, Celia Zanin-Lassila

This book is copyright under the Berne Convention
No Reproduction without express written permission.

All rights reserved. No part of this book and/or its content may be reprinted or reproduced or utilized in any form or by any electronic, mechanical, or other means, now known or hereafter invented, including photocopying, recording and programming, or in any information storage or retrieval system, without written permission from the publisher.

Notices and disclaimer

Practitioners and researchers must always rely on their own experience, context and knowledge in evaluating and using any information and methods described herein. The responsibility for using the information and methods presented are for the reader.

To the fullest extent of the law, neither the Publisher nor the Author, contributors or editors, assume any liability for the consequences of actions taken based on the content of this book resulting in damages to organizations as a matter of products liability, negligence or wrongful interpretation of the ideas presented herein.

"China is big, but it is hard."

Jeff Immelt, Chairman and CEO of General Electric

*"Real knowledge is to know the
extent of one's ignorance."*

Confucius

CONTENTS

To my mother, my sisters and the little Nina, Arno and Zora

ACKNOWLEDGEMENTS

First and foremost I would like to thank Egbert Schram, managing director of itim International , who has believed in this project from the beginning with support and enthusiasm.

I would also like to thank Jacqueline Phillips, Mel Schlein and Alfonso Tuor for reading the first draft of the book and providing me with insightful advice and suggestions.

Robert Brooks gave me invaluable help in the editing process. I have learned a lot from him and it was also a very fun experience with a lot of hysterical laughter.

Celia Zanin did an amazing job in turning my draft into a real book by showing both great taste and creativity.

I am also indebted to Paul Nichols and Matti Lehtonen for taking the time to proofread the final draft of the book.

Overall it was a great experience to work with the amazing team of itim International, where professionalism, reliability and knowledge always blend with fun and a contagious *joie de vivre*.

INTRODUCTION

There is only one thing more staggering than the mind-blowing economic and social metamorphosis undergone by China in the last few decades. It is the still widespread ignorance about China in the West and the huge gap existing between the perceptions among many Westerners of what China is and the reality of what the country has become following the most dramatic economic transformation in human history.

Almost every day China makes the headlines of the international press, yet to most foreigners it remains to many extents an unsolvable enigma. One of the main reasons for this is the fact that the coverage of Chinese affairs among many Western mainstream media outlets is often biased and incomplete, and doesn't provide a comprehensive framework able to help in untangling China's complexity.

In the blink of a generation, what only 40 years ago was one of the poorest, most backward and isolated countries in the world has become the world's second largest economy, as well as a central and influential geopolitical power. Nevertheless, despite China being closer than ever before because of the integration and interconnectedness of the world's economy brought about by globalization, to most Westerners the country is psychologically still very far away. The physical and geographical distance has been reduced through technology, business, and trade, but the mental distance is still very wide.

After years of working within and with China as a business consultant and cross-cultural adviser, I am still surprised to see how many Western businessmen keep looking at the country through some outdated and biased lenses that make it very difficult for them to truly grasp what is really going on in the world's biggest market. They might be reading the business press every day, they might be very knowledgeable, and they might have rich and extensive international experience, yet when it comes to China, many of them struggle to understand such a diverse, complex, and fast-changing reality.

Following China's economic boom of the last decades, hundreds of thousands of foreign companies, both MNC's and SME's, have flocked to the country to try to tap into the huge potential for business represented by the Chinese market. Many of them have succeeded and have managed to develop very profitable operations, but many others, including some famous global corporations, have failed miserably. In 2013, a report by Weber and Shandwick said that 48 percent of foreign businesses, including leading multinational companies, fail and withdraw from China within two years of establishing operations there.[1]

It is safe to say that the situation has not changed in the meantime, and that actually succeeding in China is becoming more and more difficult. A very telling and recent example is that of the British online fashion and beauty store ASOS, that announced in April 2016 the decision to shut down its China operations. A few weeks earlier, German online food and beverage-ordering service, Delivery Hero, operating in almost 30 countries, had announced a similar decision. In both cases these foreign players were not able to keep up with the fierce competition of domestic companies that are more able to understand the local customers and find the right ways to connect with them.[2]

These two examples are a very good case in point in showing how the market conditions have changed in China. They have changed deeply and, most importantly, they have changed so fast that it is difficult for most people who are not familiar with China to keep up with them and have a correct and well-informed grasp of what the country has become. Not only is China not what it was 10 or 15 years ago anymore, it is not what it was even two or three years ago. China is changing incredibly fast and it is changing in a combined and unprecedented way. As Lei Zhang, founder of Hillhouse Capital Management, one of China's leading investment funds, has put it, "urbanization, industrialization and the Information Age are all happening at the same time; it's like a father and son learning to drive at the same time."[3]

As a keynote speaker, in the last few years I have often been invited to corporate events to speak about China, and every time I have been surprised by the thick veil of ignorance, even among top managers of companies operating internationally, that prevents an adequate and objective understanding of the current situation in the Chinese market. Too many people still see China through some old clichés that die hard: cheap China, copycat China, low quality China, backward China, you name it. Similarly, I remember overconfident and arrogant clients coming to China thinking that their products or their technologies were the best in the world, and that the Chinese could not do anything other than roll out the red carpet for them. More often than not, they would be quickly disappointed by the realization that they had ended up in a country that was completely different from the one they had imagined.

China is in the midst of an economic structural transition of historical proportions, moving from the development model that made the Chinese boom possible after the first economic reforms launched by Deng Xiaoping at the end of the 1970's, based on low-cost manufacturing, exports and debt-driven big investments, to a new and more balanced one led by domestic consumption, innovation and the development of a modern services industry. With China moving up the value ladder, the country needs to focus more on quality and less on quantity, and the main strategic objectives laid out by the Chinese government (as shown by the 13th Five Year Plan approved in the Spring of 2016) reflect this absolute necessity.

This critical transition to a new and more sustainable growth model will certainly not be easy, and many challenges lie ahead. The road will be a bumpy one, to put it mildly, and the Chinese government will have to do much more to correct the many imbalances that characterize Chinese economy and society (not least the deep social inequalities that are rising at a worrisome rate, the alarmingly high level of debt or the lack of a modern and transparent financial system that is the indispensable condition for a full upgrade of the Chinese economic structure). But the process is well under way and it has already changed the face of China.

First, China is not cheap anymore; those looking for low-cost manufacturing now need to look to other countries such as Vietnam, Bangladesh or Indonesia. Second, while the risks of IP violation have not vanished, the days when the Chinese were only good at copying are gone. China is becoming an innovation powerhouse and giving birth to a new generation of innovative and sophisticated entrepreneurs, especially in the high-tech industries that keep gaining ground on their foreign competitors. Over the last decade, Chinese companies increased their R&D spending by more than 3000 percent[4], and now most foreign multinational corporations are facing Chinese competitors that are just as innovative or more innovative than they are[5]. Chinese companies are actually using innovation to drive their internationalization process and compete (successfully) on the global markets, as proven by Chinese global brands such as Huawei, Alibaba, Xiao Mi, Haier or Tencent.

The third big development that is profoundly changing the dynamics and the structure of the Chinese market has to do with the dramatic rise of domestic consumption. In 2015 private consumption accounted for over 66 percent of the country's GDP and Chinese consumers are becoming an increasingly powerful force both domestically and abroad. Therefore, it is essential for any foreign company that wants to be successful in China to update and upgrade its strategies. If we needed an example to show the power of the new Chinese consumer class it would be that of the 2015 edition of the Singles Day shopping holiday created by Alibaba that took place on November 11th. In just 24 hours, online shoppers spent a record 14.3 billion dollars.[6] And this in the midst of an economic slowdown and after the stock market turmoil in China that caused jitters in the world markets in the summer of 2015. One year later, the tech giant smashed a new record by reporting 17.8 billion dollars in sales, more than Black Friday and Cyber Monday combined.[7] Another mind-blowing number is the 183 billion dollars spent in 2015 by Chinese consumers on luxury products abroad, accounting for almost half of global luxury sales.[8]

The more in-depth we look into the numbers and the trends of China's consumption, the more we realize how important it is to always put all the data into the proper context in order to have a better and more objective vision of the situation in the Chinese market. By focusing solely on the numbers related to the current economic slowdown without taking into consideration the current and future consumption patterns would inevitably lead to a partial and distorted view of what is going on in China in these critical times.

For example, according to a recent report by the Boston Consulting Group[9], China's consumer economy is projected to expand by about half to 6,5 trillion dollars by 2020, even if annual real GDP growth cools to 5,5 percent, below the official target of 6,5 percent set by the Chinese government. This growth alone – fueled mostly by the new rising class of young affluent consumers and the dramatic rise of e-commerce – would be comparable to adding a consumer market 1.3 times larger than that of today's Germany or UK. The enormous opportunities that this transformation represents for consumer product companies are obvious.

As we can see, the economic and social metamorphosis of China is proceeding at a dramatic pace, and to an extent that makes it essential for anyone wishing to do business in China to have the right tools to constantly update their strategies for the increasing complexity and sophistication of the Chinese market.

Doing business in China has never been easy, but today it is becoming even more difficult, especially because of the rising costs of doing business there, the fierce competition of innovative local players, and the rapid changes of the market conditions. This does not mean that the game is over; far from it. Opportunities still abound, and success is still within reach as long as one knows how to play the game and is ready to put the right resources in place to be competitive and able to tap into the huge potential represented by an increasingly complex but also increasingly promising China.

This is confirmed for example by the annual Business Climate Survey conducted by the American Chamber of commerce in China, which is a very good gauge of how foreign companies see the situation on the Chinese market. By looking at the results of the most recent survey[10], it appears very clearly that, while the business conditions are indeed getting tougher for different reasons, China is still a top investment priority for many foreign companies, and some industries have much better prospects than others reflecting the changing dynamic of the Chinese market.

For example, the survey shows that 45 percent of

Chinese think, work, communicate or negotiate will not lead you very far.

What you need is to reach a good level of cultural intelligence that will allow you to understand the way the Chinese think and see the world, and give you the intellectual tools to adapt your behavior and your mindset accordingly. It is not an easy process; it is actually very difficult and at times very frustrating, but it is an effort that will eventually pay off and give you a competitive edge.

This book is aimed at a wider audience than the one represented by managers of companies that are doing or are planning to do business in China. Given the increasing economic clout of China on the global stage and the expansion of Chinese businesses into developed markets by way of acquisitions of companies and investments, an increasing number of people are dealing with the Chinese outside of China – whether they are new shareholders, executives or colleagues – and it is becoming therefore essential to have the right tools to be able to communicate and work more effectively with them.

My wish is that this book will be able to play at least a small part in helping you turn into success the opportunities that China represents today, and the new opportunities that will arise from the country's constant economic and social transformation.

---

[1] "Why foreign companies fail in China", 4.7.2013, http://webershandwick.asia/why-companies-fail-in-china/.

[2] http://www.tmogroup.asia/these-3-foreign-brands-quit-china-in-2016-and-heres-why/.

[3] http://insights.som.yale.edu/insights/how-do-you-invest-changing-china.

[4] http://www.strategy-business.com/feature/00370?gko=e606a.

[5] Veldohen, Steven, Peng, Bill, Mansson, Anna, Yip, George & Han, Jian, *China's innovation is going global. 2014 China innovation survey*, Strategy&, 2015.

[6] http://www.reuters.com/article/us-alibaba-singles-day-idUSKCN0SZ34J20151112.

[7] http://money.cnn.com/2016/11/10/technology/alibaba-singles-day-shopping-festival-breaks-records/.

[8] http://www.china.org.cn/business/2016-02/15/content_37786726.htm.

[9] Kuo, Youchi, Walters, Jeff, Gao, Hongbing, Wang, Angela, Yang, Veronique, Yang, Jian, Lyu, Zhibin & Wan, Hongjie, *The New China Playbook. Young, Affluent, E-savvy Consumers Will Fuel Growth*, bcg perspectives, Boston Consulting Group, December 21, 2015, https://www.bcgperspectives.com/content/articles/globalization-growth-new-china-playbook-young-affluent-e-savvy-consumers/.

[10] http://www.amchamchina.org/about/press-center/amcham-statement/amcham-china-releases-2016-business-climate-survey.

[11] KPMG Global China Practice, *China Outlook 2016*, KPMG, 2016.

[12]https://www.eiuperspectives.economist.com/economic-development/competing-across-borders.

1

—

EXPLORING CHINESE CULTURE

Our culture is the product of a combination of historical, geographical, political, military, social, natural and religious factors that, over hundreds of centuries, have come to shape the way we see, think, and organize our reality. The way we live, organize our social relationships, and conduct business is not universal, but the product of a specific cultural heritage. Most importantly, culture affects the way we think; as human beings, we are biologically generally all the same, but we do not think in the same way, and what is considered normal in one society may not be considered normal in another society shaped by different values.

This premise is essential if we want to understand Chinese culture from a Western perspective. China's historical, social and philosophical patterns have been so deeply different from those of the West that they have given way to a unique thought system. To put it simply, the Chinese do not always think in the same way we do in the West. Therefore, if we do not make a serious intellectual effort to explore the Chinese mind, we will never be able to understand China and to do business successfully with the Chinese.

If we want to understand how the Chinese mind works, and how it operates differently from the Western mind, we need to make a big jump back to the past, back to ancient China and to the cradle of Western civilization, ancient Greece. By looking at the characteristics of the Chinese and Greek societies from 2000 years ago, we can identify the social development patterns that have shaped the different cognitive models in China and in the West.

1.1. Ancient Greece VS Ancient China

According to Richard Nisbett, an eminent American cultural psychologist who has extensively studied the different thought patterns in the West and in Asia, ancient Greece was defined by two essential characteristics. The first one was the location of power in the individual. In the Greek society, ordinary people developed a unique sense of individual freedom unknown in any other ancient civilization and the "daily lives of the Greeks were imbued with a sense of choice and an absence of social constraint that were unparalleled in the ancient world" [1]. The second characteristic was the tradition of debate, which fostered curiosity and the art of rhetoric, and which was unique at the time in so far as that even ordinary people could participate in the political discussions. According to Nisbett, the strong sense of curiosity developed through the tradition of debate led the ancient Greeks to speculate about the nature of the objects and the events around them and to create causal models of them: "The construction of these models was done by categorizing objects and events and generating rules about them for the purpose of systematic description, prediction and explanation"[2].

The situation in ancient China was completely different. Instead of the sense of *personal agency* typical of Greek society, the ancient Chinese had a sense of *collective agency*, meaning that they felt that individuals "are part of a closely knit collectivity, whether a family or a village, and that the behaviour of the individual should be guided by the expectations of the group"[3]. If *individual independence* was a central tenet of ancient Greece, the Chinese counterpart was *group harmony*. Preserving harmonious social relationships was the first responsibility of any citizen, and this is why, unlike in Greece, any form of confrontation, such as debate, was discouraged.

This emphasis placed on social harmony in ancient China is due to the fact that from the beginning of its civilization the Chinese had to live in densely populated environments because of the peculiar geographical characteristics of the country. This made it necessary to find ways to live with other people in a harmonious way, such as: group discipline, impulse control, relational focus, and other psychological traits.[4] Furthermore, the Chinese were farmers and therefore needed to get along with one another, since cultivating the land requires working with other people. The context was different in ancient Greece, where most people were hunters, herders, fishers or traders, all occupations that do not require as much cooperation with others as in agriculture.[5]

Unlike the Greeks, the ancient Chinese did not develop a tradition of scientific speculation about nature and did not make formal models of the natural world, preferring to proceed by intuition and empiricism. Since the beginning of their civilization, the Chinese have been very pragmatic and never had any penchant for abstraction. They have always been more interested in the *How* than in the *Why*.

The main reason for this is twofold: on the one hand, of all the cultures born on the Eurasian continent, the Chinese civilization is the only one that has always inhabited the land that it inhabits today; on the other hand, China has been from the beginning a farming society, whose conception of time and nature was shaped by the constant and never ending alternation of the seasons. Therefore, to the Chinese the question of the origins of the world – so important for a nomadic tribe settling in a new land – did not make much sense. Actually, the impossibility for sedentary farmers to conceive a beginning of time has been such that the ancient Chinese mythology has not had any kind of legend about the creation of the world and of humanity for a very long time.[6]

The different trajectories taken by the ancient Greeks and the ancient Chinese eventually produced two very different cognitive patterns, which still shape the way we think today and that can be summarized by saying that the Western mind focuses on *things* while the Chinese mind focuses on the *relations between things*.

1.2. Analytical thinking VS Holistic thinking

The Western cognitive pattern, which finds its root in ancient Greek civilization, is normally defined as *analytical thought*, while the Asian (and Chinese) pattern is known as *holistic thought*.

Thinking holistically means focusing on the context as a whole (the "big picture"), including attention to relationships between a focal object and the field, and a preference for explaining and predicting events on the basis of such relationships. Thinking analytically means detaching the object from the context (the "detail"), focusing on attributes of the object to assign it to categories, and involves a preference for using rules about the categories to explain and predict the object's behavior. [7] Also, the holistic approach relies on experience-based knowledge, an emphasis of change, a recognition of contradiction and the need for multiple perspectives, while the analytical approach rests on decontextualizing structure from content, the use of formal logic and avoidance of contradiction.[8] In a way, while Western culture has developed concepts and models in order to separate ideas from the object (and conceptualization is a way to intellectually distance oneself to dominate reality), the Chinese way of thinking puts the emphasis on the perception of the concrete, leading to the non-development of abstract thought.[9]

At the origin of this difference in cognitive approach there is the way different cultures perceive the relationship between humanity and nature. In the Western scientific analytical tradition there is the belief that in acquiring knowledge humanity stands for the subjective world while nature for the objective world, implying therefore that nature can be separated from humanity. The opposite is true in holistic China, where humanity is seen as being an integral part of nature.[10] This is actually the main difference between the Chinese mind and the Western mind: while the Chinese emphasizes the integrity and unity of the human society and nature, the Western pattern emphasizes observation and experiment by commencing from the part to the whole.[11]

These different thinking patterns shaped by culture also have a huge impact on how people perceive things. In his cross-cultural psychological research involving participants from the United States and East Asia, Richard Nisbett has shown that Westerners are more likely to use categorization and rules in reasoning about everyday life events, while East Asians tend to focus on relationships and similarities. For example, in a study, Chinese and American children were presented with three pictures of a man, a woman and a baby and asked to pick two pictures that went together. While the Chinese tended to pick the pictures of the woman and the baby on the basis of a *relational-contextual information* ("the mother takes care of the baby"), the American children tended to group them based on *shared categories* (man and woman together "because they are adult").[12] The latter can be defined as *taxonomic categorization* (based on the perception of the similar attributes the objects may have) and the former as *thematic categorization* (based on the relationships between the objects).

The holistic character of Chinese culture is closely linked to the semantics of Chinese language, the understanding of which requires the ability to see the wider context of meaning of combined characters, and not focus solely on the single character. In fact, although a single Chinese character by itself has meaning, combining characters creates new meanings that are more than the sum of their constituent parts. It is therefore the relationship between the single characters in a wider context that create the message. Also, in order to understand a character, one has to have a complete vision of it, because a small variation in the strokes that make up the character can change its meaning completely. According to some scholars, the difference between the Western and Chinese thinking patterns can also be explained through the different alphabets, with the phonetic alphabet providing a ground for abstract and logical thought and the Chinese writing system – which is based on drawn and concrete pictorial characters – discouraging the development of abstractions.[13]

Medicine provides a very good example that shows how different the thinking perspectives are in the West and in China. In the West, doctors look for specific causes of diseases and focus on particular body components to treat. Chinese medicine treats a disease by regulating the whole body and not just a single part of it, because any disease is considered to be not only a problem in a specific part of the body but a local reflection of imbalance of the whole body. The traditional Chinese medicine holistic approach always associates localized pathology with overall body reactions. That is why the medical treatment focuses on the overall disharmony of the body rather than specific organ or body region, and most of the time the remedies are designed to restore the balance of the whole body. This means that all aspects must be considered when treating a problem and that only a comprehensive (holistic) analysis of the patients' physical condition, age, lifestyles, medical history, career, and mental state can lead to a correct diagnosis and a proper treatment.[14]

One of the consequences of the holistic character of Chinese culture is that it has shaped a thinking pattern that does not include a formal logic like the one that symbolizes the philosophical and scientific tradition of the West. This does not mean that the Chinese do not think logically; they do, but with their own kind of logic.

1.3. A holistic, paradoxical, and pragmatic culture

In order to understand how the Chinese mind works, it is essential to gain some knowledge about the main philosophical traditions that have shaped the culture of China over the centuries and that still affect the way the Chinese think and behave. One of the most important in terms of its influence and pervasiveness is Taoism, which, along with Confucianism and Buddhism, represents one of the pillars of Chinese culture.

The goal of Taoism is to reach spiritual freedom through a harmonious relationship between a human being and nature. The world and the universe have their own ways to work harmoniously in a movement of constant change; therefore humanity has no way to control nature and needs to find a way (the *Dao*) to live in harmony with it. If someone behaves in a way that goes against the natural cycles of change of the universe, he risks disrupting that harmony and causing unintended consequences.[15]

There are two fundamental principles of Taoism. The first one is that the only unchanging law of the universe is constant change. The second one is called *Wu wei* (无为), which literally means "non-activity", in the sense that a human being should not interfere with the laws of nature and force things on which he has no power. Against this backdrop, Chinese culture (shaped, as we have seen, by the unpredictable cycle of nature that, for thousands of years, has dictated the rhythm of life of a sedentary farming society) has developed a peculiar philosophy which emphasizes the fact that the world is always changing and that, therefore, the future is unpredictable and time uncontrollable.

The ever-changing nature of the world is symbolized by the law of *Yin* and *Yang*, which describes how two apparently opposite elements are actually complementary and interconnected as parts of a bigger whole that represents the harmony of the universe. The two opposite, yet complementary, elements representing the constant movement of life are bound together in a constant mutual flux, which has no recognizable beginning and no predictable end, like day and night or warm and cold. One cannot exist without the other and they keep transforming one another in a mutual relationship of change; the growth of one will cause the decline of the other (and *vice versa*), but never its demise, because the *Yin* will always have a part of *Yang* and the *Yang* a part of *Yin*.[16]

Thus for the Chinese, things will always change and what is bad today could turn to be good, just as much as a loss could turn out to be a gain in the future. The famous story of Sai Wong and his horse, learned by every Chinese in school, summarizes very well this fundamental tenet of Chinese culture. One day, one of Sai Wong's horses ran away and the neighbours came to comfort him. To their surprise, Sai Wong was not upset at all and told them that the loss of the horse could actually be a blessing in disguise. A few months later, the horse came back bringing along another beautiful and strong horse. All the neighbours came by to congratulate Sai Wong, but he caught them again by surprise by saying that receiving a horse for free could be a bad omen in disguise. One day, his son fell off the new horse and broke his leg. The neighbours went to comfort him but Sai Wong said that his son breaking his leg might turn out to be a blessing in disguise. And actually, a few days later, all the young men of the village were enlisted to go to war. Most of them died and Sai Wong's son survived because he could not be summoned due to his broken leg.

This fatalist and somehow passive relationship with time is at odds with the Western illusion to try to control and dominate time through planning and forecasts. In the West we have a *linear* conception of time, which does not take into account the past, while the Chinese see time in a *cyclical* way. For us "time is money" and we cannot afford to "waste time"; therefore we strive for action driven by the willingness to dominate events. But for the Chinese, imbued by the doctrine of the *Wu wei*, one cannot interfere with the flux of the world or pretend to change it, because this could disrupt the harmony of the universe. That is why Chinese thought does not have a "cult of *action*" as in the West, but prefers to think in terms of *adaptation* to the flux of the ever-changing world. Since human beings cannot predict the future and control time, the only thing they can do is to learn to observe the context and adapt to it, the best talent being to recognize the potential inherent in every situation in order to take the best decision by taking advantage of the best conditions available in a specific context.[17]

This characteristic of Chinese culture can be seen being played out in the business world when it comes to planning or making forecasts, representing a major source of frustration for Western business people. For example, it often happens that, even before the signing of a deal, a Western company asks its Chinese partner to prepare a sales forecast for the coming two to four years, to no avail. The fact that the Chinese do not provide the data does not mean that they do not want to; from their perspective they simply cannot, since the context could change and therefore the forecast cannot be accurate by definition. The same goes when Westerners expect Chinese to make a quick decision because they cannot afford to "waste time". As Richard Lewis has pointed out, "Asians do not see time as racing away unutilized in a linear future, but coming around again in a circle, where the same opportunities, risks and dangers will represent themselves when people are so many days, weeks or months wiser"[18].

The other important characteristic of the law of *Yin* and *Yang* is the synthetic integration of opposites and contradictions, which has been at the core of Chinese thought for thousands of years offering a "holistic and paradoxical worldview and methodology"[19]. *Yin* and *Yang* are the two contradictory forces that permeate the universe, and a person does not have to choose one over the other, but rather find his/her own balance between these two polar extreme phenomena in life.[20]

As we have seen, the opposites, like black and white, are not seen as two separate, contradictory and irreconcilable elements, but as two complementary, interconnected and interdependent parts of a bigger whole. A famous saying states that in China if a statement is true its opposite can also be true. What is certain is that the ability to integrate and manage paradoxes (or, at least, what Westerners see as paradoxes) is at the very core of Chinese culture. In the Chinese perspective, every situation, every thing, every event must always be seen in a double perspective. All events in life are interconnected, and therefore, to understand one, it is essential to understand its opposite and the dynamics of the relationship that link them together. Far from seeing a problem in the presence of two contradictory situations, this dialectic flux between opposites is actually considered to be an opportunity to get closer to the truth by producing balance and harmony between the two.

This perspective is in stark contrast with the typical binary logic of Western thought based on the principle of "non contradiction", according to which if A is true and B is the opposite of A, B must be inevitably false. It does not work this way for the Chinese, who accept that both A and B, despite being opposites, can be true. Unlike them, most Westerners are not at ease with contradictions and paradoxes and look at them in terms of clear-cut opposition rather than synthetic combination. They tend to think in terms of "black *or* white", "right *or* wrong", "State *or* market", while the Chinese see both propositions as part of a bigger perspective: "black *and* white", "right *and* wrong", "State *and* market".

We can see this cultural attribute playing out in some political concepts developed in the last few decades such as "two countries, two systems"[21] or the definition of "socialist market economy". For most Westerners, these concepts would be considered as nothing less than illogical oxymorons, but for the Chinese they are simply reflecting a holistic and dialectic integration of opposites that open the way to a new and original perspective on things; a perspective that is not based on an abstract and "ideological" analysis of reality but on a pragmatic adaptation to a specific context.

It is this intellectual predisposition that has allowed China to adopt and integrate in a very pragmatic way those Western methods, technologies, and ideas that were instrumental to China's process of economic modernization by using them in a Chinese way and without losing the cultural "Chinese core" along the way. Tony Fang and Guy-Olivier Faure explain the process in this way: "Chinese civilization is a matrix-civilization of paradoxical cultural development. China does not rigidly copy external reality or adapt to it mechanically but produces understanding and action, thus creating a new Chinese reality. (...) The process of change may be described as follows: collection of new cultural elements, sedimentation of those elements within the Chinese system, then digestion and finally re-use within the Chinese metabolism."[22]

This characteristic of Chinese thought of embracing apparent contradictions reveals itself very clearly even in the Chinese language, where we can find different words that are made up of opposite concepts. The word "thing" in Chinese is translated with *dongxi* (东西), which is the result of the combination of the words *dong*, meaning East, and *xi*, meaning West, because from a Chinese perspective everything embraces opposite properties such as East and West. Another example that speaks volumes is the word for crisis, *weiji* (危机), which is the merger of the words "danger" (*wei*) and "opportunity" (*ji*).

In the context of business, the combination of their cyclical perception of time and their ability to embrace and integrate contradictions lead the Chinese to look at every business transaction in a holistic way, taking into consideration both the benefits as well as the negative impacts, without being too much worried by the latter because things may change later. In the case of a joint venture with a Western company, they might agree with items that may be unfavourable to them in the short term (such as compromising on management structure or control of their business) if they can get the things that matter the most in the long term such as technology, capital, and know-how. Instead of looking at the unfavourable compromise as a setback, they are able to see the situation as a "win-win" for both parties.[23]

As we have seen so far, at the heart of Taoism we find the concept of harmony (harmony between opposites, between humanity and nature, etc.), which is, more generally, an essential tenet of Chinese culture, one that informs both the relationships between people and the structure of society as a whole. To find the Way (the *Dao*) means being able to achieve harmony in one's life and with the world. And to achieve this harmony the only possible way is to find a balance between opposite poles, to avoid the extremes, and to combine and integrate different perspectives by a holistic and pragmatic embrace of contradictions.

This "middle way" between extremes is reflected in the golden rule of Chinese culture called *zhongyong* (中庸) or Doctrine of the Mean. As the combination of the words *zhong* (middle) and *yong* (balance), *zhongyong* is the condition in which every proposition and viewpoint coexists without bias and prejudice. It also develops the concepts of flexibility and adaptability; a virtuous person being the one who is able to recognize what is the best and most appropriate action and behaviour in a specific context in order to achieve one's goal without disrupting natural or social harmony. It reflects, therefore, a pragmatic cultural attitude towards the world that cultivates the sense of opportunity.

The holistic and paradoxical approach of Chinese culture, combined with their relativistic conception of time as a cyclical flux that is impossible for humanity to tame, is actually the reflection of a strong pragmatism. The Chinese are allergic to models, abstractions, and absolute or universal values, which are instead so embedded in the Western intellectual and scientific tradition. Unlike Western culture, which has been shaped by the deductive approach (from theory towards practice) developed first by the ancient Greek philosophers, Chinese pragmatism is based on a purely empirical inductive approach: after having observed and tested the context, a strategy is formalized without the need to go through an abstract theory.

This pragmatist approach is epitomized by the famous ancient Chinese idiom "seeking truth from facts" that has shaped the strategies and choices of many Chinese leaders for centuries. In the early 20th century, Sun Yat-Sen, the first President and founding father of the Republic of China, said: "we cannot decide whether an idea is good or not without seeing it in practice; if the idea is of practical value to us and to the world, it is good. If the idea is impractical, it is no good."[24] Mao Zedong said the same in just a few words: "it is true what works; it is false what fails". But perhaps the slogan that comes to symbolize best the modern version of Chinese pragmatism is the one pronounced by Deng Xiaoping, the father of China's "capitalist revolution", who said that it does not matter whether a cat is white or black as long as it catches mice.

Most importantly, this pragmatism has been at the core of the Chinese "economic miracle". China did not come out of poverty and underdevelopment to become one of the most powerful countries in the world by adopting abstract and absolute theories or models. What China has done since the beginning of the economic reforms, starting with the "Special Economic Zones" – the cities and coastal regions where Deng introduced the first market reforms in the early 1980's before extending them to the whole country –, is to build its success through a trial-and-error approach. A gradual approach consistent with the traditional pragmatism of Chinese culture that is quite different from the one adopted in many Western countries. While China starts with experimentation and with pilot projects on a small scale and, if successful, subsequent extension to other areas, in many Western countries reforms start with constitutional amendments (often preceded by very ideological debates) followed by changes in laws and regulations and implementation. As a top Chinese public intellectual and former interpreter for Deng Xiaoping has said, the success of China is not dependent upon a deduction of value-based truths, because the Chinese place practice-based truths above value-based truths, and this has not only created an economic miracle but also redefined perhaps some truths that the West has always taken for granted.[25]

1.4. A collectivistic and hierarchical society

China has always been a rural society where family was the basic social unit. These two aspects combined have shaped Chinese culture and society around "collectivistic" values. Unlike in most Western cultures, where individual freedom and independence are the most important values, in China the individual can express himself only in the wider context of a group or a community by always avoiding behaving in a way that may disrupt social harmony.

As we have seen already, the fact that the ancient Chinese civilization was a highly densely populated country and a farming society, requiring people to get along in order to work together on the land, had forced the Chinese to find ways to preserve social harmony, the latter becoming much more important than any form of individual autonomy. The fact that in this ecological context the family came to play a central role in the Chinese social organization has further strengthened the importance of the group and of group harmony. The centrality of the group in Chinese social organization is symbolized by the fact that, in China, unlike in the West, people write first their family name and not their first name. Belonging to a clan is therefore traditionally much more important than individual identity to the extent that the Chinese language does not even have words for the concepts of *identity* and *personality* in terms of a person separate from the context.[26]

Against this backdrop, group orientation has become a central aspect of Chinese culture, which attempts to cultivate an interconnected sense of self, meaning that individuals subordinate themselves to the group to sustain a social order and stability.[27] This is one of the reasons why a Chinese person is not encouraged to think in an individualistic manner or attitude as in the West. To a Chinese person, self-fulfilment is tied to the sense that they are in harmony with the wishes of their group and are meeting the group's expectations. As in any collectivistic society, the Chinese "self-esteem is not linked to the individual but to relationships with others"[28].

Having said that, the radical, deep, and extremely rapid economic and social changes experienced by Chinese society in the last few decades raise the question whether China is becoming more "individualistic". Rapid urbanization, increased wealth, interaction with the West through travel or studies abroad, is certainly having an impact on many Chinese, especially those of the younger generations. Some research actually shows that younger Chinese are more individualistic than older ones and are more likely to live according to their own lifestyles and less likely to follow the traditional collective ideology.[29]

While this is true to some extent, we cannot fall into the typical ethnocentric trap and interpret these results as evidence that the Chinese are becoming more Western-like. First of all, culture is a very complex mental structure made up of different layers, some visible some not. If we look at culture as an onion, we can see in the outer layers the more superficial spheres, which can be related to social practices such as fashion and consumption, for example. The young Chinese might drink Coca-Cola and dress in famous Western brand clothes, but does it mean that they are starting to think as Westerners do? The answer is negative, because when we look at the deeper layer of the "culture onion", at the sphere of values (the fundamental feelings about life, people and society that we learn when we are children and are so embedded in us that most of the time they guide our behaviour subconsciously), we realize that the young Chinese are still very different and are still very much more collectivistic than young Westerners.

Chinese society, like many other societies in the world, is undergoing rapid change but there is no evidence so far that the values of present-day generations from different countries are converging.[30] As has been rightly pointed out, "self-expression is not equal to independence of thought", while personal success and gratification in China "is still synonymous with societal acknowledgment"[31].

The present situation cannot therefore be misunderstood as a linear and inevitable shift from collectivism to individualism in a Western sense, because in China the influence of the group and of society is still very important and much more important than it is in the West; the phenomenon should be seen, therefore, in its full complexity, by reasoning "within a double entry system in which the individual approach moves through the collective sphere and vice versa"[32].

The same holds true for another central characteristic of Chinese culture and society, which is strictly correlated and intertwined with collectivism: hierarchy. Since the beginning of its civilization, China has been a strongly hierarchical culture with strict and rigid hierarchical rules that apply to every social organization, and that is rooted in the principle of unequal relationships among people. In its history, China, more than any other civilization in human history, has for centuries been under constant threat of invasion from the nomadic tribes of the Asian Steppe, from which the Chinese population had no natural protection. This persistent and aggressive pressure from outside led the ancient Chinese to accept the authority of strong rulers and highly centralized unified states for much longer than just about anywhere else in the world.[33]

The organization of Chinese society and the Chinese state along a very rigid hierarchical code is the result of the political and philosophical thought of Confucius (551-479 BC), whose philosophy has shaped Chinese culture over 2000 years of history by emphasizing the importance of maintaining a strict and well-defined hierarchy in order to achieve and preserve harmony within the society. Confucius codified a highly hierarchical and vertical social order that continues to influence and shape social relations in China.

Other evidence attesting the centrality played historically by the family in Chinese culture is that the "Confucian social order" is based on the traditional Chinese familial organization. What makes Confucianism particularly different from the Western tradition is the primacy placed by Confucius on loyalty to parents over every other obligation in society and the extreme lengths to which familial relations evolved under his influence. For Confucius, if the family is strong, peaceful and harmonious, then all of society will be just as much. In the opposite case, if families were in disorder, all of society would similarly fall into chaos.[34]

According to Confucianism, the absolute preconditions for familial, and therefore social, harmony are *obedience* and *loyalty* to the parents, which are the pillars of the Confucian concept of "filial piety" called 孝 (*xiào*). In the Confucian perspective, *xiào* is the foundation of all other virtues and the basis of proper social behaviour in all aspects of life: if a child reveres his parents, he will also be a loyal citizen and an honourable gentleman. [35] Based on this idea, Confucius created a strict social order consisting of five basic human relationships that he ranked in order of subordination: sovereign-subject, parent-child, husband-wife, elder brother-younger brother and elder friend-younger friend. In this hierarchy of social relations, everyone has been assigned a very clear role that it is essential to respect in order to preserve social order and harmony.

Nevertheless, while for Confucius it is essential to respect this very strict hierarchical organization of family and society, obedience and loyalty to one's king, father or boss is not unconditional and unilateral. Another important element of Confucianism is the fact that the relationship between higher and lower hierarchical ranks is one based on *reciprocity*. It is true that a son must be loyal and obedient to his father; but in turn the father must be caring and provide his son with security, protection, and benevolence. The same is expected from the government with regard to its citizens. In exchange for their loyalty and obedience, the ruler must act as a strict, severe, yet "benevolent father".

Despite the many twists and turns of Chinese history, this strictly hierarchical order has been a permanent and central tenet of Chinese society that still shapes social relationships even today. In the business world, for example, notwithstanding the deep social and economic shifts undergone by China in the last few decades, generally speaking management tends to be more paternalistic than in Western companies, with the boss acting like a strict yet benevolent father and employees usually exhibiting a higher degree of devotion to the company than Western workers, provided that reciprocity is respected.[36]

Despite the rapid changes in Chinese society, and the fact that these changes are certainly having an impact on the values of the Chinese population, especially among the new generations, the deep cultural structures and codes of China are still very much valid today, because "we are speaking about changes, about an incredible evolution, but not about a swing or an inversion of values"[37]. Therefore, while there is certainly a partial and gradual adaptation to the new realities of modern China, the collectivistic and hierarchical characteristic of Chinese culture still represent a major difference with Western cultures and still shape the way the Chinese think, see, and organize their world.

[1] Nisbett, Richard E. et al., « Culture and Systems of Thought : Holistic Versus Analytic Cognition », in *Psychological Review*, 2001, Vol. 108, No. 2, p. 292.

[2] *Ibid.*

[3] *Ibid.*

[4] Bains, Gurnek, *Cultural DNA. The psychology of globalization*, Wiley, Hoboken, 2015, p. 163.

[5] Nisbett, Richard E., *The Geography of Thought. How Asians and Westerners Think Differently…and Why*, Nicholas Brealey Publishing, London-Boston, 2010, p. 34.

[6] Javary, Cyrille J.-D., *La souplesse du dragon. Les fondamentaux de la culture chinoise*, Albin Michel, Paris, 2014, p. 20.

[7] Nisbett et al., *op. cit.*, p. 293.

[8] *Ibid.*

[9] Faure, Guy Olivier, « China : New Values in a Changing Society », *Euro China Forum*, http://www.ceibs.edu/ase/Documents/EuroChinaForum/faure.htm.

[10] Li, Ma, « Epistemological Reasons for Lack of Science in Ancient China », in *Open Journal of Social Sciences*, 2015, 3, p. 168.

[11] Xu, Xiuyan, « Cultural Factors in EAP Teaching – Influences of Thought Pattern on English Academic Writing », in *Cross-cultural communication*, 2012, Vol. 8, No. 4, p. 54.

[12] Nisbett, Richard E. & Miyamoto, Yuri, « The influence of culture : holistic versus analytic perception », in *Trends in Cognitive Sciences*, Vol. 9, No. 10, October 2005, p. 467.

[13] Ji, Li-Jun, Nisbett, Richard E. & Zhang, Zhiyong, « Is It Culture or Is It Language ? Examination of Language Effects in Cross-Cultural Research on Categorization », in *Journal of Personality and Social Psychology*, 2004, Vol. 87, No. 1, p. 58.

[14] http://www.shen-nong.com/eng/principles/holism.html.

[15] Fasching, Darrell J. & deChant, Dell, *Comparative Religious Ethics. A Narrative Approach to Global Ethics*, Wiley, Hoboken, 2001, p. 35.

[16] Javary, *op. cit.*, p. 64.

[17] Jullien, François, *Traité de l'efficacité*, Grasset, Paris, 1996, pp. 88-89.

[18] Lewis, Richard, « How Different Cultures Understand Time », in *Business Insider*, 1.6.2014, http://www.businessinsider.com/how-different-cultures-understand-time-2014-5?IR=T.

[19] Faure, Guy Olivier & Fang, Tony, « Changing Chinese values : Keeping up with paradoxes », in *International Business Review*, 2008, No. 17, p. 196.

[20] Wee, Chow-Hou & Combe, Fred, *Business Journey to the East. An East-West Perspective on Global-is-Asian*, McGraw-Hill, Singapore, 2009, p. 56.

[21] This doctrine was developed by Deng Xiaoping in the early 1980s with regard to the relationship between the People's Republic of China and Hong Kong and Macau. It stated that, while being part of communist China, the two regions could retain their own capitalist system.

[22] Faure & Fang, *op. cit.*, p. 206.

[23] Zhang, Haihua & Baker, Geoff, *Think Like Chinese*, The Federation Press, Annandale, 2013, p. 16.

[24] Schell, Orville & Delury, John, *Wealth and Power. China's long march to the Twenty-First Century*, Random House, New York, 2013, pp. 8-9.

[25] Zhang, Weiwei, *The China Wave. Rise of a Civilizational State*, World Century, Hackensack, 2012, p. 91.

[26] *Ibid.*, p. 185.

[27] Shuang, Liu & Chen, Guo-Ming, « Assessing Chinese Conflict Management Styles in Joint Ventures », in *Intercultural Communication Studies*, IX-2, 2000, p. 72.

[28] Mooij de, Marieke and Hofstede, Geert, « Cross-Cultural Consumer Behavior : A Review of Research Findings », in *Journal of International Consumer Marketing*, 23 :p. 183, 2011.

[29] Zeng, Rong & Greenfield, Patricia M., « Cultural evolution over the last 40 years in China : Using the Google Ngram Viewer to study implications of social and political change for cultural values », in *International Journal of Psychology*, 2015, Vol. 50, No. 1, p. 48.

[30] Hofstede, Geert, Hofstede, Gert Jan & Minkov, Michael, *Cultures and Organizations. Software of the Mind*, McGraw Hill, New York, p..

[31] Doctoroff, Tom, *What Chinese Want. Culture, Communism, and China's Modern Consumer*, Palgrave Macmillan, New York, 2012, p. 235.

[32] Faure & Fang, *op. cit.*, p. 201.

[33] Bains, *op. cit.*, pp. 163-164.

[34] Schuman, Michael, *Confucius And the World He Created*, Basic Books, New York, 2015, p. 103.

[35] *Ibid.*, p. 104.

[36] *Ibid.*, p. 187.

[37] Faure, *op. cit.*

2

＝

MEASURING CHINESE CULTURE

Having explored the way the Chinese think by looking at the fundamental pillars of Chinese culture and thought, it is now important to start considering how to put this knowledge to use in a business context. In the next chapters we will see how the Chinese cultural codes have an impact on the way the Chinese communicate, negotiate or deal with business management and organization. But first we need to put Chinese culture in a broader context by comparing it to other cultures in order to "measure" it. Knowing Chinese culture is important, but even more important is to understand in which way this culture is different from others and how these differences have an impact on business. Once we can determine where and how cultures differ in dealing with a specific matter or situation, it is easier to identify some patterns of behaviour, which, in turn, can allow us to predict problems and give insights on how to deal with them.

In order to do that, we will use the famous cross-cultural model developed by Dutch social psychologist Geert

Hofstede, who in 2008 was included by the *Wall Street Journal* in the list of the world's most influential management thinkers. His model – which is the result of pioneering and seminal empirical and statistical research started in the late 1960s, and further developed, replicated, enriched, and upgraded right up to the present day – was one of the first to adopt a pragmatic problem-solving approach by directly relating culture to management and is one of the most widely used worldwide in the field of intercultural management. Hofstede's Model gives us a set of very useful tools to predict potential cross-cultural conflicts and misunderstandings, and to put in place adequate measures to prevent them. It is, therefore, a very good instrument for anyone dealing with China.

The model is the result of Hofstede's theory of cultural dimensions that analyses and describes national cultures along six dimensions reflecting different social situations or problems. Every dimension represents a scale between two poles on which every culture can be ranked and then "measured" in relation to another culture's score. The six dimensions of Hofstede's model are the following: Power Distance, Individualism *vs* Collectivism, Masculinity *vs* Femininity, Uncertainty Avoidance, Long-term orientation *vs* Short-term orientation and Indulgence *vs* Restraint. In the following pages, we will apply this model to Chinese culture to see how it ranks within each dimension and to compare it to other cultures. This way, we will have a much broader and clearer picture of the Chinese cultural codes in a comparative framework, which will allow us then to proceed to a more detailed analysis of the impact that Chinese culture has on business.

2.1. Power Distance

The Power Distance dimension refers to the different ways of coping with inequality and represents the "extent to which the less powerful members of institutions and organizations within a country expect and accept that power is distributed unequally" [1]. The Power Distance Index (PDI) measures, therefore, not the degree of inequality in a society, but the way people feel about it. In a country with a low PDI, then, most people expect power relationships to be rather democratic and egalitarian, while in a high-PDI country the less powerful members of society accept their position and the existence of rigid and formal hierarchical structures.

On the Power Distance scale, China ranks very high (a score of 80 out of 100), which means that most Chinese believe that inequalities among people are acceptable. Generally speaking, such a high score in PDI has the following consequences in the relationships of power between people of different ranks:

- the subordinate-superior relationship tends to be polarized and there is no defense against power abuse by superiors;
- individuals are influenced by formal authority and sanctions and are in general optimistic about their superiors' capacity for leadership and initiative;
- people should not have aspirations beyond their rank. [2]

2.2. Individualism vs Collectivism

The second dimension in Hofstede's model refers to the

degree of individualism in a society. According to Hofstede, in *individualistic societies* everyone is expected to look after him- or herself and their immediate family, while in *collectivistic societies* people from birth onward are integrated into strong, cohesive in-groups, which throughout people's lifetime continue to protect them in exchange for unquestioning loyalty.[3]

As we have already seen, China is a strongly collectivistic country and scores very low (20 out of 100) on the Individualism index (IDV). In fact, China is one of the most collectivistic countries in the world, based on Hofstede's ranking. Such a low score means that in China:

- people act in the interests of the group and not necessarily of themselves;
- in-group considerations affect hiring and promotions with closer in-groups (such as family) getting preferential treatment;
- employee commitment to the organization (but not necessarily to the people in the organization) is low;
- where relationships with colleagues are cooperative for in-groups, they are cold or even hostile to out-groups.
- personal relationships prevail over task and company.[4]

2.3. Masculinity vs Femininity (or Assertiveness vs Modesty)

This dimension focuses on the extent to which a society stresses achievement/success or cooperation/care. According to Hofstede, Masculinity emphasizes ambition, material success, assertiveness, acquisition of wealth, power, strength, and individual achievements. The opposite pole, Femininity, emphasizes cooperating and caring behaviours towards other people, gender equality, modesty, quality of life, and more fluid gender roles.

With regards to work and business environments, on the masculine/assertive pole we find societies where priorities are getting a high salary, being recognized when a good job is done, pursuing career advancements and having a challenging job giving a personal sense of accomplishment. On the feminine pole we find other priorities: having a good working relationship with your direct superior, working with people who cooperate well with one another, living in an area desirable to you and your family, having the security that you will be able to work for your company as long as you want to.[5]

With a score of 66 on the Hofstede scale, China is a Masculine society (MAS), therefore, success oriented and driven. The need to ensure success can be exemplified by the fact that:

- many Chinese will sacrifice family and leisure priorities to work;
- service employees will provide services until very late at night;
- leisure time is not so important;
- the migrated farmer workers will leave their families behind in faraway places in order to obtain better work and pay in the cities;
- Chinese students care very much about their exam scores and ranking as this is the main criterion to achieve success or not.[6]

2.4. Uncertainty Avoidance

The Uncertainty Avoidance dimension refers to the degree

of tolerance that a society has for ambiguity and the way such a society deals with the fact that the future can never be known: should we try to control the future or just let it happen? This ambiguity brings with it anxiety and different cultures have learned to deal with this anxiety in different ways.

Cultures with a high Uncertainty Avoidance Index (UAI) do not like ambiguous and uncertain situations and try to minimize them through strict codes of behaviour and laws, while low-UAI cultures are much more at ease with uncertainty and tend to have fewer rules and laws.

At 30 China has a low score on the Uncertainty Avoidance Index. This result is in line with the characteristics of Chinese culture outlined in the previous pages. According to Hofstede, this low score means, in fact, that in China "adherence to laws and rules may be flexible to suit the actual situation and pragmatism is a fact of life"[7]. Furthermore:

- the Chinese are comfortable with ambiguity;
- the Chinese language is full of ambiguous meanings that can be difficult for Western people to follow;
- Chinese are adaptable and entrepreneurial.

2.5. Long-term vs Short-term Orientation

This dimension refers to the relation that a specific culture has with the past and the way it deals with present and future actions and challenges. It is particularly interesting when used to measure the differences between Western and Asian countries.

According to Hofstede, countries that score low on the Long-Term Orientation index (LTO) are short-term oriented and prefer to maintain time-honoured traditions and norms while viewing societal change with suspicion. On the other hand, those that score high on LTO take a more pragmatic approach and encourage thrift and efforts in modern education as a way to prepare for the future.[8]

In this dimension China scores very high (87), which means that it is a very long-term oriented and pragmatic culture with the following characteristics:

- people believe that truth depends very much on situation, context, and time;
- they show an ability to adapt traditions easily to changed conditions;
- they have a strong propensity to save and invest;
- they are thrifty;
- they show a strong perseverance in achieving results.

2.6. Indulgence vs Restraint

The sixth and last dimension of the Hofstede model is defined as the extent to which people try to control their desires and impulses, based on the way they were raised. Relatively weak control is called *Indulgence* and relatively strong control is called *Restraint*.[9]

Indulgent societies tend to allow relatively free gratification of natural human desires related to enjoying life and having fun, whereas *restrained* societies are more likely to believe that such gratification needs to be curbed and regulated by strict norms. Indulgent cultures tend to focus more on individual happiness and give more importance to leisure time and personal freedom. On the other hand, in restrained cultures positive emotions are less freely expressed and happiness, freedom, and leisure are not given the same importance.

With a low score of 24 on the Indulgence *vs* Restraint

scale (IVR), China is clearly a restrained society. Societies with a low score in this dimension have a tendency towards cynicism and pessimism. Also, in contrast to indulgent societies, restrained societies do not put much emphasis on leisure time and control the gratification of their desires. People with this orientation have the perception that their actions are restrained by social norms and feel that indulging themselves is somehow wrong.

2.7. Comparing cultures

What is very important to always keep in mind is that, since Hofstede's model is conceived for cross-cultural comparisons, the scores of a country (in this case China) along the 6 dimensions cannot be read and analysed by themselves in absolute terms, but always in relative terms by comparing them with the scores of another country.

To give a concrete and recent example, in January 2015 the Chinese group Anbang acquired the Dutch insurance company Vivat for 150 million Euros. Only two months after the completion of the deal, in September 2015 the Dutch CEO of the company resigned from his post because of a cultural clash in leadership, management, and governance style.[10]

As we can see in Figure 1, if we compare Chinese and Dutch cultures by using the Hofstede model, it is clear that on almost all dimensions (with only the exception of the LTO dimension, where the gap is less pronounced) China and the Netherlands find themselves on opposite poles and, without a proper intervention, the cultural clash that led to the resignation of the Dutch CEO was inevitable.

It is clear that if the Chinese group had done an in-depth and professional *cultural due diligence* by using a model like Hofstede's, it could have seen from the outset that the operation was bound to face many problems, and that in order for it to be successful a cross-cultural assessment of the merger leading to a proper cultural adjustment strategy was absolutely necessary.

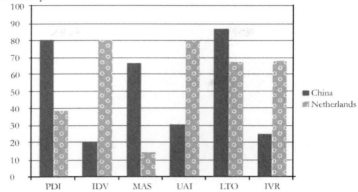

Figure 1

2.8. *Culture clusters*

What makes Hofstede's model a very good and useful tool for any company doing business across different cultures is also the fact that by combining some of the dimensions together we can identify some cultural clusters that reflect different organizational and management cultures.

According to Hofstede there are six main cultural clusters:

- "Contest": countries with low PDI, high IDV, high MAS and low UAI (Western English-speaking countries).
- "Network": countries with low PDI, high IDV, low MAS and medium UAI (Netherlands and Scandinavian countries).
- "Family": countries with high PDI, low IDV, medium MAS and low UAI (e.g. China and India).

- "Pyramid": countries with high PDI, low IDV, medium MAS and high UAI (e.g. Mexico, Portugal, Russia).
- "Oil machine": countries with low PDI, high IDV, high MAS and high UAI (e.g. Germany and Austria).
- "Solar System": countries with high PDI, high IDV, medium MAS and high UAI (e.g. France and Belgium).

The Chinese culture, combining a high Power Distance, a low Individualism, a medium high assertive and competitive tendency with a low UAI, is part of the Family cluster, whose main characteristics are as follows:

- The privilege to define new priorities and directions lies at the top of the organization.
- The leader of the company is supposed to indicate what he sees as the common interest for all insiders in the company.
- The implicit expectation is that the person at the top has a complete overview of what is happening and from such a position can decide what the right decision is.
- Once the decision is taken, the leader must be clear in cascading down the new mandates giving unambiguous directions.
- The visibility of the commitment of the person at the top is essential.
- The employees expect the top management to be concerned about the in-group interest and to be willing to protect the in-group in the change process.

After this long but necessary overview of the main pillars of Chinese culture and their contextualization with regards to other cultures, in the next chapters we will see how these Chinese cultural codes affect the way the Chinese work, organize, communicate, negotiate, manage, and do business. Through the information provided so far, it will be easier to capture the main characteristics of Chinese culture and get the right perspective for helping to navigate the complexity of Chinese business.

---

[1] Hofstede et al., *op. cit.*, p. 61.

[2] http://geert-hofstede.com/china.html.

[3] Hofstede et al., *op. cit.*, p. 92.

[4] http://geert-hofstede.com/china.html.

[5] Hofstede et al. *op. cit.*, p. 139.

[6] http://geert-hofstede.com/china.html.

[7] *Ibid.*

[8] *Ibid.*

[9] *Ibid.*

[10] « Culture clash behind surprise resignation of Vivat boss, 15.9.2015, http://www.dutchnews.nl/news/archives/2015/09/culture-clash-behind-surprise-resignation-of-vivat-boss/.

3

三

KEY CONCEPTS OF CHINESE CULTURE

One of the central characteristics of Chinese culture that make it so different from most Western cultures is its collectivism. Unlike the Western individualistic cultures that put individual autonomy and self-expression at the heart of their social structure, in China the individual is always seen only as an element of a bigger whole, whether it is the family, the company or society at large. In short, while most Western societies are individual-oriented, the Chinese society is group-oriented. This aspect of Chinese culture is essential to understand for any Western business person planning to do business in China, because it has a huge impact on business relationships and organization. Underestimating it, or worse, ignoring it, would seriously affect any chance of doing business successfully in the Chinese market.

This collectivistic feature of China is reflected in two key concepts of Chinese culture in general and of Chinese business culture in particular, whose importance cannot be overstated: *guanxi* (关系) and *mianzi* (面子). As we will see, these two concepts are strictly interwoven and represent somehow the linchpin of Chinese social relationships. To many Western business people in their first business or working experience in China, the insistence on these concepts might sound odd, but it is not. If one really wants to lay the groundwork for success in the Chinese market, it is essential to understand that underestimating *guanxi* and *mianzi* would be a serious and costly mistake.

3.1. Guanxi

If there is one thing that is fundamental to always bear in mind when doing business or working in China, it is that China is a relationship-based society and therefore *relationships come before business and not the other way around*. This is especially difficult to understand for business people coming from very individualistic cultures, who are mainly focused on the business or the transaction at hand. To them, business comes first and before any other kind of consideration. Then, if after a deal is signed there is the chance to develop a personal relationship with their partner, it is fine. But certainly, considering the development of a good human relationship with a potential partner as a precondition to doing business together almost amounts to nonsense to many Westerners.

But this is actually the way people do business in China, and not being able to properly adapt to this completely different mindset will almost certainly preclude the chances of being successful in the Chinese market. The saying "business is business, friendship is friendship" does not apply to China, where business and friendship are expected to merge and generate a long-term relationship that goes beyond the specific business at hand.

The importance of personal relationships in business in China is symbolized by the concept of *guanxi*. *Guanxi* is often translated as "network" or "connection", but it means much more than that; it is the web of relationships that a person builds throughout his/her life, and it encompasses more than the simple business relationships by including family or friendship ties at large. The importance of *guanxi* in China must be understood in the historical frame of a traditionally rural society where, for centuries, there was a lack of formal institutions and laws that made it essential to rely on personal relationships to organize and structure social life.

Literally *guanxi* is the combination of the words *guan* (关) and *xi* (系), meaning respectively "closed" and "connection"; it means therefore a *close relationship* between two people but also a *closed relationship*, which means that for outsiders it is not easy to become part of their *guanxi*. In order to be accepted into an existing *guanxi,* one has to gain the trust of its members, and building trust takes time and requires some concrete proofs (read favours) that the person can be trusted and welcomed into the network. But it goes beyond that; *guanxi* is more than a network based on mutual interests, because it must involve a strong human and emotional component. *Guanxi* is actually strictly dependent on the concept of *renqing* (人情), which translates literally both as "human feelings" and "favour" and dictates that the human element should never be removed from any human affair, business and working relationships included, and that understanding and a sympathetic give-and-take should govern the relationships of people.[1]

Guanxi is, therefore, very different from the Western-style business networking, where companies' common interests prevail over individual personal relationships. Both in China and in the West, trust is essential to build an effective and reliable network, but the concept and nature of trust is not the same in both contexts. According to Francis Fukuyama, in China trust must be seen as "in-group" trust at the personal level, while Western culture is characterized by a "system trust" built up at the impersonal level, which means that while in Chinese business culture trust is *interpersonal*, in the West it is *inter-organizational*.[2]

This is a fundamental element of *guanxi* that cannot be neglected or misunderstood: the business relationship is always personal, between two persons, not between companies or organizations. This means that, when preparing for doing business in China, any Western business person will always have to remember that his future partners, counterparts, colleagues or employees will not do business or work with his company, but with him *personally*.

Another tenet of *guanxi* is reciprocity, which means that a strong and effective business network cannot be built without a mutual exchange of favours. If someone provides some kind of assistance to another member of his/her *guanxi*, the latter is expected to reciprocate in some way sooner or later. The favour does not necessarily have to be business-related, given that *guanxi* is relationship-oriented and not transaction-oriented. For example, if a Western businessman could help his prospective Chinese business partner find a good school for his children in Europe, and organize all the arrangements without asking anything in exchange, it would most definitely open him the way to the *guanxi* of his business partner, who would feel compelled to reciprocate in one way or another. Therefore, *guanxi* could be seen as an informal community based on trust and loyalty, which can open many doors and offer many opportunities as long as the obligation of reciprocity with no limitations of time and space is respected.

Three things are sure when it comes to building *guanxi*. First, without *guanxi* there is no way to do business effectively in China. Since China is a relationship-based society, building strong relationships with the right people is essential and can bring many benefits in terms of building corporate reputation, obtaining new customers, motivating employees, improving marketing effectiveness, easing business processes or improving business efficiency in the Chinese market.[3] Second, regardless of the intrinsic value of a specific business deal, having a better *guanxi* than the competitors with the right people in the right position gives a strong competitive advantage. Third, and last but not least, building a good *guanxi* takes a long time. If a Western businessman expects to enter the Chinese market for a quick buck and then leave as soon as possible, he better think again.

For anyone who is planning to do business in China, is looking for a business partner or who is about to start a negotiation with a Chinese counterpart, the first thing that he/she must do is to build trust, which is the lifeblood of *guanxi*. But building trust in China takes time, especially for a Western business person. Impatient business people or managers who think their product or their technology is so good that building relationships is not necessary will most certainly face a painful disappointment. Once again, in China, relationships come before business and there is no shortcut to that. That is why patience is one of the most valuable skills when dealing with the Chinese market.

One thing that is very important to stress is that, in order to build the right connection, the relationships need to be cultivated outside of the business setting. And if this means taking part in many dinners and social events that involve a lot of drinking, it is important to participate with an open mind and a good predisposition. In this context, it is always essential to remember that *the real relationship is not between companies but between people.*

Since building a *guanxi* takes time and involves a good amount of socializing, it is obviously easier to develop it for someone who is based in China. For the others, they need to understand that, if the Chinese market represents for them a priority that requires an investment in resources, people, and time, a couple of trips a year are not enough. Different visits need to be planned in order to build a good relationship with a potential partner. And in the common case where a Western company relies on an advisor based in China to help develop its business there, the latter can certainly lay the groundwork in terms of building the first connections and preparing the preliminary phase of a potential deal. However, when a counterpart or a potential partner has been identified, the person in charge of the deal must go to China and plan as many visits as is necessary in order to establish a personal connection.

For many Westerners, especially for those used to getting "straight to the point" who do not like to "waste time" in matters that are not strictly business-related, it will be very difficult to accept the idea that before becoming partners in business, the Chinese want to be friends with them. It is something very difficult to understand especially for the most individualistic cultures, such as the American one, whose identity is based on the *individual* rather than on the *relationships between individuals* as in China. Two different perspectives have been compared by using the metaphor of the spider web: in China the personality is the web, representing the different fibres attaching to significant others, while the American is the spider, traveling along the fibres for his own purposes.[4] But the spider strategy in China simply will not work. Certainly, building a good relationship with a Chinese business partner based on mutual trust will take time, but, once the doors of his *guanxi* are open, the chances of developing a successful business venture will increase exponentially.

In this context, it is essential to understand a central feature of Chinese business culture, one that many foreign business people ignore or underestimate to their own detriment: most believe that the personal relationship with a business partner develops after a contract is signed, while the Chinese believe that *there needs to be a relationship before a contract gets signed.* They believe that, since personal relationships are the best way to build trust, they should take precedence over legal and formal documents. This is why putting too much pressure on a counterpart to sign a contract because "time is money" and you need to catch the flight back home, without having established a good personal relationship beforehand, will most probably lead to problems that could affect the whole business.

In China, the very essence of a transaction is not legal but relational, and if a Chinese counterpart does not trust you yet because you have not established a personal connection, your insistence to sign a contract could only inflate his suspicions. This is really where you clearly see the biggest differences between the Chinese and the Western business cultures being played out. The Chinese way of doing business tends to start with relationships (feelings and emotions), followed by logic (reasoning) and finally legality (contracts), while the Western approach works exactly the other way around.[5]

Another very important point that needs to be made is that a person's *guanxi* is strictly personal and therefore non transferable. It is not inheritable. Therefore, if the manager of a foreign company in China has been able to establish an important and wide business network along his many years spent in the country, when he leaves his post his *guanxi* will not automatically be transferred to his successor. That is why, for example, when it comes to negotiation, it is important that the negotiating team that established the relationship with the

Chinese counterpart from the beginning will not be changed along the way. This personal element of *guanxi* is critical and must be taken into serious consideration by any company planning to develop a business venture in China. As we have said, building a *guanxi* is essential and it takes a long time to establish a good one, but the problem is that, today, many companies tend to shorten the time of the assignments of their managers in China. An assignment which is too short could actually prevent the firm from establishing the right *guanxi* and therefore limit the potential for success in the Chinese market.

The collectivistic and relational elements underpinning the dynamic of *guanxi* are as ancient as China, but their application can be very modern indeed by also proving very useful in business and commercial contexts that go far beyond the personal dual relationship between two persons doing business together. For example, recent research has shown that the huge success of Taobao, the online shopping website owned by the Alibaba Group, is also partly due to a specific strategy of creating a *guanxi* with the customers to foster brand loyalty. When they purchase online, the customers of Taobao are encouraged to have live chats, which are very popular; this experience has not only increased the amount of purchases on the website, but more importantly, has created a personal connection between Taobao and its customers, because the conversations and feelings that were shared during the interactions resulted in a form of *guanxi*, which is likely to translate into customer loyalty.[6]

As we have seen, *guanxi* is a central tenet of Chinese business culture because China is a relationship-based society, where the human and personal elements play a more decisive role than in most Western countries. It is therefore essential for any company planning to do business in China to integrate the development of the right *guanxi* in their wider market-entry strategy. Certainly, it takes time and effort to build a *guanxi*, and it takes even more time and effort to maintain it, but it is an investment that will eventually pay off and give an important competitive edge.

3.2. Mianzi

Another core element of Chinese culture that has a huge impact on business and work relationships, and that is strongly interconnected with *guanxi*, is the one of *mianzi* (面子).

Mianzi means "face", in the sense of "losing face". But it has a very different meaning than in Western culture. In fact, while in the West "face" is associated with guilt, in China (and, more generally, in Asia) it is related to shame. This difference is quite relevant, because guilt reflects an individual dynamic between the individual and his own conscience, while shame relates to a social context where the individual feels ashamed because he has infringed on the rules of his group, and therefore affected its harmony. While guilt is felt regardless of whether the misdeed is known or not by others, shame is felt only if the infringement is known by others.[7] And this cultural factor is a central and critical part of the social fabric of China.

Therefore, while preserving one's face is a universal concern, in China it has a much greater significance than in the West, and the main reason for that is related to the necessity of preserving social harmony, which, as we have seen in the previous chapter, is one of the most important elements of Chinese culture. Since the beginning of Chinese civilization, people lived in rural communities with very restricted geographical mobility, which made it necessary to maintain harmonious relationships among members of the community and to avoid conflict and confrontation at all costs. In that context, preserving face was therefore very important.

Furthermore, Confucius emphasized that, since humans exist in interactive relationships with others, and that these relationships need to be harmonious to preserve social stability, accepting and respecting each person's need to maintain his or her face was essential to preserve social harmony.[8] Therefore, if social harmony is achieved through controlling emotions and behaviour in order to avoid the disruption of group harmony and hierarchies, those who do not follow this code of behaviour would be considered as losing face and shameless.[9]

If we want to simplify, in China a person's "face" represents somehow his reputation; prestige or status in the eyes of others within multiple social contexts such as the family, the company, the circle of friends and society at large; it is somehow the sum of the person's social worth[10]. Being a collectivistic society, the Chinese are almost obsessed by their reputation, to the extent that – as we will see in the following chapters – sometimes preserving one's face is more important than telling the truth, which can have quite a few consequences in cross-cultural business and work relationships. It is common, for example, for someone not to admit having done something wrong because this admission would make him lose face. For the same reason, in the workplace there could be an employee who, after making a mistake that will almost certainly cost him his job, resigns first rather than losing face by getting fired.

While this obsession with "face" might seem weird to many Westerners, it is really essential to always remember that the importance of preserving *mianzi* in China cannot be overstated. As a famous Chinese idiom says, "you can kill me, but you cannot insult me". In China, a person's reputation rests on saving face, and making someone lose face – even if unintentionally – can be disastrous for business negotiations or work relationships. For example, one of the golden rules to respect in China is to never lose one's temper in a meeting and adopt an aggressive and arrogant attitude; this would make the Chinese hosts lose face and almost certainly compromise a fruitful cooperation in the future. In order to preserve one's own face and other people's face, it is really important to always treat people with respect and consideration and to behave in a proper and well-mannered fashion.

To illustrate this, I always use an example that I personally experienced a few years ago, and that many foreign consultants have certainly experienced at some point in time. A client of mine wanted to export his technology to China and was looking for a potential Chinese partner to do business with. After having identified a few potential companies, I organized an intense week of meetings around China, and I warned my client that he had to be prepared for a business environment that was completely different from the one he was used to. The problem was that, despite my warnings and my insistence on the fact that in China relationships come before business, his expectations were completely unrealistic and could have never been met. He was expecting to go back home, if not with a contract, at least with a formal promise to work together, which, as we have already seen, is almost impossible regardless of the intrinsic value of the deal at hand.

After realizing that the Chinese were not on the same page as him, and were not ready to go straight to the point and talk about details and numbers in a first meeting, he completely lost his temper and started shouting at them by pointing his finger and accusing them of making him lose time. They did not budge and kept smiling, but obviously the deal was already dead before even being discussed. By losing his temper, by confronting the counterpart directly and aggressively and putting them on the spot, by not showing the proper respect to his hosts, my client caused a loss of face and, eventually, the loss of a potentially interesting business.

What is very interesting and fascinating about the concept of *mianzi*, is the fact that, since face is a person's social status and reputation asset, as an asset it can be traded. This means that I can "give face" to someone in order to increase his reputation and then he will be compelled to reciprocate sooner or later. For example, giving face is very important in the process of establishing a *guanxi*, because giving someone face (by praising him publicly, through gifts or invitations to lavish banquets or by making concessions in a negotiation, for example) can be very effective in the process of building relationships and influencing decisions.

In the following chapters, we will see how the importance of the concept of *mianzi* in Chinese culture translates into different business and working contexts, especially with regards to employees' management, communication style, and negotiation strategies.

The bottom line is that preserving face is crucial. If you are able not only to respect your Chinese counterpart- or employee's face, but also to enhance it, your chances of success will increase. On the contrary, if you make your Chinese counterpart or your employee lose face, even if you did not intend to, you could seriously damage or condemn your respective business prospects and affect the productivity of your company.

SUMMARY

GUANXI – THE CRUCIAL ROLE OF RELATIONSHIPS

- In China relationships come before business and not the other way around.
- A relationship needs to be built before signing a contract and not the other way around.
- The business relationship is always personal: the Chinese do business with you, not with your company.
- *Guanxi* is strictly personal. If you build a strong *guanxi,* and then leave China, your successor will not automatically inherit it.
- Reciprocity is a central tenet of the Chinese system of both personal and business relationships.
- Without *guanxi,* doing business in China effectively and successfully is very hard, if not impossible.
- Having a better *guanxi* than your competitors will give you a strong competitive advantage.
- Building a good *guanxi* takes a long time. Patience is essential to do business in China.
- To build a strong relationship based on mutual trust with a Chinese counterpart, it is essential to plan many trips to China and also engage in many non business-related social events.

MIANZI – THE IMPORTANCE OF PRESERVING FACE

- The concept of "face" in China is associated with shame and not with guilt like in the West. Therefore face is lost in front of other people.
- The Chinese are almost obsessed by face. In some situations it can seem absurd, but you need to accept it and act accordingly.
- Making someone lose face – even if unintentionally – can be disastrous for business or work relationships.
- Never lose your temper in a meeting and adopt an aggressive and arrogant attitude. Always treat people with respect and consideration and behave in a proper and well-mannered fashion.
- Always try to "give face" to your Chinese counterparts or business partners; it will strengthen your *guanxi*.

1 Chu, Chin-ning, *The Asian Mind Game. Unlocking the hidden agenda of the Asian business culture – A Westerner's survival manual*, Rawson Associates, New York, 1991, p. 237.

2 Yin, Fei, « An Analysis on Factors of Success for Chinese/European JVs in Culture Aspect », in *International Journal of Business and Management*, Vol. 3, No. 6, June 2008, p. 9.

3 Yang, Fang, « The Importance of Guanxi to Multinational Companies in China », in *Asian Social Science*, Vol. 7, No. 7, July 2011, p. 165.

4 « Bridging Cultural Divides : Doing Business in China », in *The World Financial Review*, 28.5.2014, http://www.worldfinancialreview.com/?p=1862.

5 Wee, Chow-Hou & Combe, Fred, *Business Journey to the East. An East-West Perspective on Global-is-Asian*, McGraw-Hill, Singapore, 2009, p. 139.

6 Wee, Chow-Hou, « An Integrative Perspective on *Guanxi* : Dispelling Myths to Facilitate Business in China », in *Global Business and Organizational Excellence*, Vol. 34, Issue 1, November/December 2014, p. 62.

7 Hofstede, Geert, Hofstede, Gert Jan & Minkov, Michael, *Cultures and Organizations. Software of the Mind. Intercultural Cooperation and Its Importance for Survival*, McGraw-Hill, New York, 2010, p. 110.

8 Wei, Xiaohong & Li, Qingyuan, « The Confucian Value of Harmony and its Influence on Chinese Social Interaction », in *Cross-Cultural Communication*, Vol. 9, No. 1, 2013, p. 64.

---

[9] Faure, Guy Olivier & Fang, Tony, « Changing Chinese values : Keeping up with paradoxes », in *International Business Review*, Vol. 17, 2008, p. 198.

[10] Turner, Stephen P., *How to Win in China. Business and Negotiation Strategies Revealed*, L&T Publishing, Austin, 2011, p. 40.

4

四

PEOPLE MANAGEMENT IN CHINA

Given the cultural idiosyncrasies of China, Human Resources Management continues to top the list of business challenges for foreign companies operating in the Chinese market. If a foreign company wants to build an effective team able to develop a successful business, it needs to understand that it is essential to adapt its practices and models to the new cultural environment. Applying to the Chinese market practices and models that have proven effective before without adjustment to the new cultural paradigm will almost certainly lead to problems that will eventually affect the efficiency and effectiveness of the organization.

But this is only part of the picture. Actually, the cultural factor is only adding another layer of complexity to a situation that is already quite challenging because of the specific problems of the Chinese employment market that make it quite difficult for any foreign company to recruit, develop, motivate, and retain employees.

The first problem is the shortage of talent. In China, the fast development and modernization of the economy, along with the resulting rise of labor costs, has not been matched by an equivalent increase of competences. According to a recent survey, 8 out of 10 executives of foreign companies operating in China consider talent shortage a risk for their business development to the same extent as the country's economic slowdown, and far more important than other factors such as regulatory framework, domestic competition, financial instability or copyright violations.[1] Another research shows that, despite a massive increase in the number of students graduating from Chinese universities over the last 15 years, in 2013 more than a third of employers in China surveyed said they struggled to recruit skilled workers, with 61 percent of these companies attributing this to a shortage of general employability skills.[2]

Compounding the challenge for foreign companies, more Chinese firms, both private and state-owned, are gaining prestige and setting foot on the international stage. They are also enjoying a better reputation among workers, which means that foreign firms will face greater challenges in finding the talent they need to help them achieve their business objectives.[3] In the past, foreign firms were by far the preferred choices for Chinese employees thanks to their connectedness with the global markets, their reputation and, last but not least, their salaries, which were much more appealing than the ones paid by Chinese companies.

Now the situation is changing, and foreign companies need to cope with very aggressive domestic competition for talent. Chinese companies, especially private ones, are investing heavily in attracting the best professionals by providing very competitive wages and career prospects that, in some cases, are more appealing than the ones offered by foreign firms. Remuneration is particularly attractive at senior management level and beyond, when it reaches or even exceeds the salary levels common in more mature economies such the US or Europe.[4] Furthermore, what makes Chinese companies more interesting to Chinese professionals is the fact that they are considered to provide more opportunities for substantial career advancement than international companies. According to a report by the recruitment company Michael Page, published at the end of 2015, 80 percent of Chinese employees would consider joining a Chinese company.[5]

The combination of these factors, and given the fact that the employee-turnover rate in China is particularly high for international standards[6], means that the competition amongst Chinese companies to get the top talent will increase. This will make it essential for any new foreign company planning to go to China to be ready to put in place the right resources to create a context able to appeal to the best and the brightest in the Chinese market.

But obviously, in order to be able to do so, a foreign company needs to include in its China development plan a proper and adequate cross-cultural strategy that allows for adjusting HR strategies and models in such a way that they can fit effectively the cultural peculiarities of the Chinese market.

Certainly, without proper cross-cultural training, a foreign manager, especially if coming from the West, will inevitably face many problems, seemingly absurd situations, and a lot of misunderstandings when dealing with Chinese employees. Therefore, only a comprehensive HR management strategy that tackles the increasing competition for talent with a proper cultural adaptation strategy can pave the way for a successful venture in the Chinese market. Underestimating the local competition in the race to get the best professionals, and neglecting the cultural factor would more likely lead to failure rather than success.

4.1. Managing Chinese employees and the importance of "face"

The different way of thinking and of seeing reality of the Chinese, coupled with the collectivistic and highly hierarchical character of Chinese society, creates such a peculiar cultural environment that it becomes essential for foreign managers to change their views on how to manage people by adapting their models to the Chinese reality. For Western companies especially, just sticking to the way they are used to working in the West will simply lead them nowhere.

When talking with people who have had experience in people management in China, these are the most common remarks that one will hear:

- In China the employees are often reluctant to say what they think.
- Managers are expected to give orders and employees are expected to follow them.
- Chinese employees usually lack initiative and wait to be told what to do.
- Chinese employees usually do not think "outside of the box", are not proactive, and lack an aptitude for risk-taking.
- An employee generally does what is asked, nothing more and nothing less.
- Staff will never object to a decision of their boss, even if it is a wrong one that could affect the business.
- People usually do not bring up problems for fear of losing face.

All of these statements are true. Obviously, there are always exceptions depending on different factors, but these are situations that, in general, will be likely to arise.

It is definitely true that, usually, among Chinese employees in China it is difficult to find the same degree of initiative, individual self-expression, and proactivity as in the West. The first reason is that, starting from their childhood within their family, Chinese are raised to always follow instructions from the top, and are used to a much more hierarchical structure in which each person has a clearly defined role. The second reason is that the Chinese education system teaches students to respect conformity instead of fostering independent thinking. On the one hand, Chinese education has always been focused on rote learning instead of promoting critical and independent thinking and questioning things. On the other hand, given the high Power Distance of Chinese society, in the structure of Chinese schools the teacher is always right and cannot be questioned. Students, therefore, are not used to raising their hands to ask a question or to state an opinion.

Within such a system, it is obvious that cultivating soft skills very useful in the business world such as creativity, proactivity, risk-taking, leadership, spirit of initiative, and teamwork are not easy to develop. Therefore, any foreign manager preparing for an assignment in China needs to take this context into serious consideration and be prepared to profoundly adapt his management strategy to a completely different reality, because he will inevitably face situations that would have been unconceivable to him back home. This adaptation process will take time and will definitely not be easy, because it involves the ability to really reconfigure one's mindset and basic assumptions about people management.

For example, if a foreign manager is used to involving staff in the decision-making process by asking for his employees' opinion, or if he is used to leading meetings where everyone is encouraged and willing to speak out and to share their ideas, he cannot expect the same to happen automatically in China.

In a Chinese company, it is generally considered inappropriate for employees to express their opinion in a meeting unless they are asked to by their boss. Offering one's opinion without invitation is actually often interpreted as a lack of confidence in the manager or even as an act of insubordination that would make the manager lose face.[7]

Even more inappropriate would be for employees to openly express opinions different from those of their superiors. In fact, even when they think that their boss is wrong because his decision could be detrimental to the company's strategy, Chinese employees tend to agree with him because of the fear of making him lose face. In the case that there would be something really important that really needs to be discussed, the employee would talk to the superior and express his opinion, but exclusively in private, not in front of his colleagues, in order to preserve the manager's face.

Another typical situation likely to happen is when a manager asks, in a team meeting, for ideas or suggestions to solve a problem; if anyone dares to speak, most likely they will not fully speak their mind so as not to embarrass themselves with ideas that may be rejected, or out of fear that these ideas could be contradicting the manager's opinion.

To a foreign manager, especially one coming from a very individualistic and low Power Distance Western culture, this insistence on preserving "face" at almost any cost can be really unnerving, obscure, if not absurd, but it is really at the very core of working relationships in China. As we have seen before, the importance of harmony, and the resulting need to preserve face, is one of the tenets of Chinese culture. Therefore, both senior executives and employees have an obligation to avoid making the other person lose face, because preserving face means preserving the harmony in the workplace.

For this reason, in any kind of critical situation involving a specific employee or colleague, care must be taken to deal with it in a "face-safe" environment, meaning that the manager must talk to him face-to-face, and not in front of other colleagues. Therefore, if a manager needs to talk to an employee to criticize his work, if he does not want to make him lose face (and, with it, any motivation) he needs to talk to him in private. Research has shown that giving negative feedback to a subordinate in a harsh and blunt way may make the employee lose face, which may block further communication between the manager and the subordinate; also, negative feedback on job performance could in some cases generate feelings of resentment, which may produce mistrust that may even make the employee quit.[8] The same goes if the manager wants to get some ideas from his staff. Since employees are generally expected to remain silent and to speak only when asked to, the best way to solicit suggestions and honest opinions is to talk privately with each of them.

Another critical point when it comes to managing people in China is that usually Chinese employees avoid making decisions outside their role and responsibility for fear of violating, once again, the balance and harmony in the workplace. It is therefore essential that any work assignment be extremely detailed and very specific, with each individual task or role clearly defined. Chinese are good workers and they will complete tasks effectively as long as they are clearly defined in order to avoid any room for ambiguity and misunderstandings.

This is a very important point to take into consideration. A foreign manager might be used to giving assignments without getting involved in the small details because these are considered implied and it is expected that the employee be flexible and proactive enough to deal with them without the need for any additional instruction. Thinking that this attitude would automatically work in China would very likely lead to frustration. When giving instructions to a Chinese employee, especially at the early stage of a working relationship, any detail that is considered important must be explicitly stated, even though "common sense" would make us think that that same detail is obviously implied in the context and does not need to be told.

But nothing is implied in China. The language and cultural differences are already a significant source of misunderstandings; therefore it is essential to keep any potential additional misunderstanding to a minimum by being as clear and detailed as possible. Every task must be clearly stated and care must be taken so that the employee has clearly understood what his responsibility is and what the management's expectations are. A good piece of advice is to set tasks, responsibilities, and expectations in written form. If it is not clear whether the employee has fully understood his task, the manager should talk to him in private and make sure that he does.

Given this context, in order to increase effectiveness, foreign managers should get involved in tasks at the beginning, clearly define the role for each employee, and constantly monitor progress to make sure that the project as a whole is on track. In many Western countries, such a degree of involvement of a manager would be seen as unnecessary "micromanagement". But, in order to guarantee the success of a project in China and to avoid that something gets "lost in translation", at least at the beginning of a working relationship, micromanagement is essential.

Because of inexperience or the fear of making a mistake and therefore losing face, employees usually want more guidance and direction from the management on how to do their job and are more likely to look to the boss for detailed instructions. Research has shown that in China most employees "prefer direct and precise instructions, especially from someone at the top" and that "they depend on such individuals to clarify work issues whenever ambiguity arises"[9]. Another study has confirmed that most Chinese employees prefer a situation where job instructions are comprehensive and strictly followed rather than be broad and allowing employees to determine how to complete the job.[10]

Therefore, in order to avoid any pitfalls due to ambiguity and confusion as to the responsibilities of each employee, and the risk of being bothered every time a small problem arises, it can be very useful to outline in a written document in a very clear and detailed way the guidelines regarding the job description and the expected performance standards.

When it comes to problem solving (and in any business venture in China there will definitely be many problems along the way), it is not enough to just ask employees to think about a solution. In order to actually get some real feedback from an employee, the request must be formalized and structured. It should be a formal assignment, with a clear goal and a clear schedule. The employee must understand that his role is to think about any kind of idea that could help solve the problem, and that he must do it within a specific deadline. When the proposals are ready, they will be discussed only with the manager face-to-face, in order to avoid "face saving"-related pressure or embarrassment.

4.2. Chinese leadership style: the "benevolent manager"

In the context of Chinese people management, a very important point that needs to be made is that, when it comes to the relationship between executives and employees in China, one must be very careful not to misunderstand the dynamics of Chinese hierarchy.

On the one hand, it is true that the management structure in China is much more hierarchical and much less democratic than in most Western countries. Despite the modernization of the economy and the society, and the resulting trend towards more individualism among the younger generations, China is still a high Power Distance society where most employees tend to prefer an authoritative leadership style. This style of leadership fosters a prescriptive, clear, controlled environment, and can be reassuring for younger middle management and the professional workforce that is not yet comfortable in dealing with the complexity of business management in a Western-style, consensus-driven and matrix-based environment.[11]

On the other hand, this does not mean that the boss holds absolute power and that he can do whatever he wants without considering his employees' opinions and feelings. In China, the boss is not a dictator, but rather a "benevolent father". And the principles and codes underlying the Chinese management style could be defined as "paternalist management".

This is a good example of the influence that Confucianism still has on the cultural and social fabric of China. The social order shaped around the thought of Confucius is based on the hierarchical structure of the family and on the relationship between father and son; a relationship that is replicated in every kind of hierarchical order in the society, whether it is between the citizen and the State, the teacher and the students or the manager and the employees. And this hierarchical structure is based on loyalty and obedience. The son must be loyal to his father and always obey to his orders. However, this relationship needs always to be considered in a context of reciprocity, meaning that, if the son must be loyal and obedient to his father, the latter must ensure consideration, respect, and protection to his son.

The same goes for the relationship between a manager and his employees. The manager is usually seen as a benevolent leader, who mixes a paternal care for staff with clear expectations and hard discipline, like the typical good father of the typical Chinese family. This is very important to bear in mind for any manager assigned to lead and manage Chinese employees. Especially because, while in most Western countries HR management mainly focuses on processes, in China it focuses on the people.

This is why, in order to start building a *guanxi* with his employees, a foreign manager must be ready to give part of his free time to non-work related social activities (dinners, parties, karaoke,...) aimed at creating a good atmosphere among colleagues as if it were a big family. This is very important: in China, relationships within the company need to be built also outside of the office and the work hours by making the employees feel part of something bigger that goes beyond their daily professional tasks. It is essential to understand that a company's loyalty to its employees counts first; only then employees will also develop feelings of loyalty towards the company.[12]

But obviously, in order to create a sense of belonging among the employees a few dinners out or company parties are not enough. What employees are looking for, especially among the younger generations, is to have a clear sense of the goals of the company and the feeling of being part of a collective effort to reach those goals. It is therefore essential to build a corporate culture that allows the employees to identify themselves with the company's aspirations and objectives.

According to a recent survey, the most important aspects of corporate culture for most Chinese employees, especially among the younger generations, are a clear vision of the company's direction, respected leadership, governance, and the belief in fairness and promotion on merit. In this context, a company needs, therefore, to go a long way to create a context where a diverse and dynamic workforce can feel that they can fulfil their professional and personal goals.[13]

4.3. Motivating and retaining Chinese employees

Due to the shortage of talent, recruiting the right people in China is not an easy task, but what is really difficult is to retain them. Retaining people is not just about pay or providing opportunities for advancement; it is also about creating a workplace that engages the whole person. For many Chinese, in fact, the company is as much a social community as a place of work. Therefore, a good manager must be able to find an appropriate balance between results and tasks and the welfare of employees.

Given that China is a collectivistic and relationship-based society, the Chinese generally tend to distrust strangers, those who are not part of their *guanxi* or "in-group". Anyone who is an "out-group" needs to gain their trust before being able to work effectively with them. Managing employees in China is a particular challenge because loyalty is primarily directed to the in-group, which is normally represented by the wide circle of family and friends, unless the company's general manager succeeds in creating a family feeling within his company by building up personal relationships with his employees.[14]

In this context, it is essential for foreign managers to go a long way to gain the trust of their employees. It is true that Chinese employees accept and expect a high Power Distance between them and their boss, but they will execute their assigned tasks with commitment and efficiency only if they trust their manager. And this process of building trust starts by showing that the management cares for them.

For example, taking interest in workers' families and personal lives is a good way to show respect and empathy, and is very important in order to be considered a good boss in China. As in any business relationship with the Chinese, one thing that always works is to show a genuine interest for their culture, their family and so on. A new foreign manager who would act in an arrogant and distant way and only focus on tasks without any kind of personal and human empathy towards his employees would definitely have a hard time creating the appropriate level of *guanxi* with the staff in order to be able to get the best out of it.

Obviously, though, even in China showing empathy to the employees is not enough to motivate them. One must find the right incentives, and, as we have seen, retention of employees in China is a very serious challenge for any company. The question of employees' motivation is sensitive, given that, for decades, reward systems and other motivational factors have not been a natural part of the Chinese organization and society. One needs, therefore, to be able and flexible enough to adjust his motivational tools to fit the specific organization.

Moreover, what triggers the motivation of employees is not the same everywhere in the world and therefore one cannot simply replicate the models used in the West. It is essential to understand what motivates people in a specific culture and adapt accordingly, because what motivates a person coming from a very individualistic country like the United States can be very different from what motivates someone coming from a very collectivistic country like China.

For example, a very popular motivational program like the "Employee of the month" can work very well in the US, because it is shaped by a very individualistic culture that values individual accomplishment and performance above anything else. But such programs do not work necessarily well in collectivist cultures, where it is very uncomfortable for the individual to be singled out of the group. In collectivistic societies, if the reward is too individualistic and bottom-line oriented, it may create pressure for the recipient and his group, which could negatively impact the relationship between team members. A recent study on performance appraisal practices in China has shown for example that in some cases if one team member keeps gaining the highest rating, even if he is really better than the average the risk of jealousy and conflict within the team is really high, and therefore the managers tend to avoid situations that can damage the balance and harmony of the group.[15]

In China, individual motivation is therefore often somehow related to a group dimension. This is why team awards are very appropriate, because they please employees who want to feel part of a larger frame of success. This does not mean that individual awards cannot be taken into consideration. If someone clearly excelled and deserves to be thanked, he should be; but it is important to contextualize his recognition in terms of his contribution to the team. Though the need for recognition is high, too much praise for any one individual could disrupt group harmony.

The ideal reward scheme should be able to combine both individual performance as well as that of the team. In fact, in devising the proper motivational strategies, a manager needs to perform a constant balancing act between the need to drive high performance on the one hand and preserving group harmony and face on the other one. As for everything in China, maintaining balance is always the key.

When it comes to finding the right incentives to motivate and retain employees, it is important to show flexibility in order to adapt to the fast changing context of Chinese society and to take into consideration the different generational, hierarchical, geographical or personal factors that make up such a big and complex country.

Generally speaking in China, still to some extent an emerging economy, employees tend to value a good and stable income more highly than in the most industrialized Western countries, where other more "qualitative" factors are taken into consideration.

This is particularly true for the youngest workers, who are in a stage of life when they need to buy a house (a very important status symbol in China) or to start a family, while, at the same time, having to provide for their parents and grandparents. For these reasons, to them money is obviously more important than an interesting job. Also, if these young Chinese live and work in big and very expensive cities, like Shanghai, housing benefits can also be a very important motivator, not necessarily so in the second- and third-tier cities, where the cost of apartments is much lower.[16]

These are the main factors that should be taken into consideration when it comes to young employees at the beginning of their career. But if we talk about managers or employees with very rare and highly competitive skills, even if a good salary is still important, there are many other incentives that can help the company retain its best talents.

Different studies and surveys have recently shown, for example, that senior executives value recognition and respect more than salary, while junior executives tend to base their employment decisions on total rewards, future career opportunities and establishing a balance that allows for quality of life.[17] Generally speaking, while salary is still the most important motivator for employees in China, including managers, other factors such as career promotion and development, development of personal goals, work/life balance are becoming more important especially among employees with a university education.[18]

In this context, foreign firms face increasingly stronger competition from Chinese companies at all levels, because, on the one hand many domestic companies offer now very competitive and highly favourable compensation and benefits packages, and, on the other hand, they have a strong competitive advantage when it comes to important motivation factors such as career development and advancement.

While salary is still the most important motivator, for many Chinese employees, especially among the younger generations and the better educated, career prospects are becoming more and more important and to many of them Chinese companies offer better prospects than foreign ones. According to a recent survey, almost 60 percent of Chinese employees cite better long-term career progression and promotion opportunities as the reason to work for a Chinese company.[19] Actually, one of the top reasons for employee turnover is the lack of real and significant career development opportunities and many Chinese employees leave foreign companies because they feel that they have reached the "bamboo ceiling" and that top promotions are reserved only for expats.

Therefore, for a foreign company to be competitive in the battle for talent in China, it needs to break these "glass ceilings" and develop long-term career development paths that include a real opportunity to advance up to the top executives posts in the company. Especially when it comes to highly-skilled managers, they will be more likely to stay in the company in the long term if they see a serious prospect for personal and professional development that includes the opportunity to reach the top echelon of the corporate ladder. For these reasons, promoting within the company, setting clear and achievable goals for employees at all levels (i.e. executive management included), and having a mentor program are all initiatives that can increase the levels of employee morale and motivation.[20]

Against this background, any foreign company that is planning to operate in the Chinese market needs to seriously consider two main factors. First, when it comes to talent management in China, a "one-size-fits-all" strategy cannot work. The regional differences, with different levels of economic development, and the differences between generations, with their different aspirations and goals, call for a very flexible and adaptive approach. An approach that is made even more necessary by the incredible speed of change in Chinese economy and society. Second, China is not cheap anymore, and without an appropriate investment that is suitable for the evolution of the Chinese employment market, the chances for success are close to zero. China is moving up the value chain, and so are Chinese employees. They know what they want and they know where they can find it, and today, as we have seen, a foreign company is not necessarily the most interesting employer anymore.

This is why, in order to be competitive and lure the best and the brightest (who, as we have seen, are still a limited pool of people compared to the size of the Chinese population), a foreign corporation needs to put in place the right resources that allow them to offer comprehensive career prospects that, besides providing adequate salaries, wages, welfare packages, and different benefits, include training and mentoring programs, international experiences, and, most of all, the real opportunity to rise to the top.

This last point is very important to consider, not only in terms of attracting the best performing and skilled professionals, but also in terms of the wider long-term prospects of the company's business in the Chinese market and its ability to build this success on a culturally intelligent strategy.

Given the central importance of building long-term relationships when doing business in China, it is important for a manager to live and work in China long enough to be able to create these relationships and then leverage them. The problem is that in many cases the assignments of expatriates are not long enough to reach this goal. Also, as we have seen, *guanxi* is between people and not between companies, which means that a foreign manager's *guanxi* is not automatically inherited by his successor. At the same time, the constant rotation of managers has an impact on the perception that Chinese employees have of the long-term commitment to China of the company they are working for and can affect their sense of loyalty towards the organization.

Besides all these factors, the costs of executive expatriates in China continue to rise due to the increasing cost of living and the dramatic problem of pollution; compensation packages are swelling and, on average, today a total package for an expatriate middle manager in China is worth over $276 000.[21] This means that, while China is still a popular expat destination, it looks like attracting talent from abroad is getting more difficult than what it used to be. In 2014, for example, according to UniGroup Relocation, twice as many people moved out of China than into the country.[22]

In this context, it appears clear that, in order to lure top managers to China for a 3-5 year assignment and reduce the risk of assignment failure to a minimum, the option would be to invest more than less. But, as we have seen, the costs are becoming really important, which would be even more so in case of early returns. For companies that have a serious and long-term commitment towards developing their activities in the Chinese market, and are ready to devise a comprehensive strategy that reflect this commitment both in financial and operational terms, one possible solution to this problem of rising costs of expats would be to attract top local talent and groom them to become the next leaders of the company in China. By working with them on a comprehensive and detailed career development plan, they would grow within the company, absorbing its culture and developing their skills with clear prospects in terms of vertical advancement.

By putting in place the right resources to develop a pool of talents selected to become the next leaders of the company in China, a company would be able to reduce the cost of expats while leveraging the strong points of local leaders, namely their familiarity with the local culture and their personal *guanxi*. In an increasingly complex and fast changing China that requires strategic flexibility and cultural intelligence, a foreign company that is able to find an adequate combination and integration of foreign and local talents that can bring the best out of a culturally diverse environment, will be able to create the right ground to set foot in China for the long run and build a lasting and successful operation.

SUMMARY

- Preserving face is at the core of Chinese working culture.
- HR management focuses on people and not on processes.
- It is generally considered inappropriate for employees to express their opinion in a meeting unless they are asked to by their boss.
- Employees do not publicly express opinions different from those of their superiors.
- If a manager needs to criticize an employee or give negative feedback, he must do it in private, and not in front of other colleagues, to preserve the employee's face.
- The best way to solicit suggestions and honest opinions from employees is also to talk privately with each of them.
- Any work assignment needs to be extremely detailed and very specific, with each individual task or role clearly defined.
- Set tasks, responsibilities and expectations in written form.
- At least at the beginning of a working relationship micromanagement is essential.
- In China the boss is not a dictator, but a "paternalistic manager" who mixes a paternal care for staff with clear expectations and hard discipline.
- Building a good relationship with employees is essential. Participating in many social activities outside the office and after working hours is a good way to establish a good *guanxi* with the staff.

- Show interest in workers' families and personal lives.
- Motivational programs should combine individual performance rewards with team rewards.
- While salary is still the most important motivator for employees in China, other factors such as career promotion and development or work/life balance are becoming more important.
- To win the battle for talent, a foreign company must give Chinese managers a real opportunity to advance up to top executives posts.

[1] « Les paradoxes de la gestion des RH », in *Connexions*, Hiver 2015-2016, p. 48.

[2] Chen, Li-Kai, Mourshed, Mona & Grant, Andrew, *The $250 billion question : Can China close the skills gap ?* , McKinsey & Company, May 2013, p. 7.

[3] « Winning in China : Building Talent Competitiveness », Manpower Inc., November 2010, p. 3.

[4] *Global Mobility: Moving the right people to the right place at the right cost. A collection of White Papers from the 2014 Expatriate Management Conference,* Mercer, p. 28, https://www.imercer.com/uploads/GM/qol2015/pdf/Global-Mobility-Moving-the-right-people-to-the-right-place-at-the-right-cost.pdf.

[5] *2016 Greater China Employee Intentions Report*, Michael Page, October 2015, p. 25.

[6] In 2013, for instance, 35 percent of Chinese staff employed at international companies had changed jobs in the past two to four years, while 10.4 percent of them had found a new job within the previous year. See: « Employer Branding in China : Attracting Chinese Employees », in *China Briefing*, http://www.china-briefing.com/news/2015/07/28/employer-branding-in-china-attracting-chinese-employees.html.

[7] Wang, Jia, Wang, Greg G., Ruona, Wendy E. A. & Rojewski, Jay W., « Confucian Values and the Implications for International HRD », in *Human Resource Development International*, Vol. 8, No. 3, September 2005, p. 320.

[8] Chen, Jie & Eldridge, Derek, « Are standardized performance

appraisal practices really preferred ? A case study in China », in *Chinese Management Studies*, Vol. 4, No. 3, 2010, p. 253.

[9] Cheng, Kevin H. C. & Cascio, Wayne, « Performance-Appraisal Beliefs of Chinese Employees in Hong Kong and the Pearl River Delta », in *International Journal of Selection and Assessment*, Vol. 17, No. 3, September 2009, p. 331.

[10] Cai, Z., Morris, J. & Chen, J., « Explaining the human resource management preferences of employees : a study of China workers », in *The International Journal of Human Resource Management*, Vol. 22, Issue 16, 2011.

[11] Raynaud, Christine & Eagan, Angie, « Company Culture in Building a Strong and Stable Workforce in China », *China Business Review*, 8.11.2013, http://www.chinabusinessreview.com/company-culture-in-building-a-strong-and-stable-workforce-in-china/.

[12] Roth, Hans J., « Personnel Management in China », *Swiss Re Centre for Global Dialogue*, 26.5.2015, http://cgd.swissre.com/risk_dialogue_magazine/Talent_in_China /Personnel_Management_in_China.html.

[13] 2013 *MRIC Talent Report* – Greater China Region and Singapore, p. 17.

[14] *Ibid.*

[15] Chen, Jie, *op. cit.*, p. 252.

[16] Flisak, Daniel & Bjerkhage, Thomas, *How culture affects the motivation of employees. A study in differences in motivation between Swedish and Chinese employees*, Bachelor Thesis 15HP, University of Gothenburg, School of business, economics and law, June 2015, p. 45.

[17] Nie, Winter, « Talent management in China : It is not one-size-fits-all », *Swiss Re Centre for Global Dialogue*, 26.5.2015, http://cgd.swissre.com/risk_dialogue_magazine/Talent_in_China/Talent_management_in_China_It_is_not_one-size-fits-all.html.

[18] Yang, Fang, « Work, motivation and personal characteristics : an in-depth study of six organizations in Ningbo », in *Chinese Management Studies*, Vol. 5, No. 3, 2011, p. 286.

[19] *2016 Greater China Employee Intentions Report*, Michael Page, October 2015, p. 26.

[20] Chmielecki, Michal, « HR Challenges in China », in *Journal of Intercultural Management*, Vol. 4, No. 3, September 2012, p. 52.

[21] Nylander, Johan, « Expat Pay Is Getting Fatter in China », *Forbes*, 20.5.2015.

[22] « Twice As Many Expatriates Leaving China Than Arriving, Moving Company Says », *The Wall Street Journal*, 9.2.2015.

5

五

COMMUNICATION

In the era of globalization there is no successful cross-border business without effective cross-cultural communication. The fact is that communicating effectively across cultures can be sometimes a daunting challenge. It requires the ability to get out of one's own cultural comfort zone to try to understand how other people from other cultures see and perceive reality.

The writer Anaïs Nin once said that we do not see things how they are, but how we are. We all look at reality through our own special cultural glasses that distort the perception of things. This is why, in order to be able to communicate effectively with people with other cultural codes and perspectives, it is essential to try to look at the world with their eyes, because the reality might be the same, but the perception of it changes depending on the people's cultural standpoint. And since communication is all about perception, what

99

matters is not the message, but how it is perceived. This is true in any cross-cultural encounter, but even more so in China, where the communication style can sometimes represent a huge challenge for foreigners, especially if coming from the West.

The way the Chinese communicate is actually one of the most difficult, and often frustrating, things for many foreign business people to get used to. Getting "lost in translation" in China is very easy without a proper cross-cultural training. But the real difficulty is not necessarily about the language differences and the fact that Mandarin is very difficult to learn and master, because communication is not just about language; it is much more than that.

Today, especially in the big cities and among the younger generations of professionals, in many cases language in itself is not a problem anymore. We can find many Chinese business counterparts, partners, colleagues or employees who can speak decent or fluent English, which means that on a superficial, linguistic level we may think that we understand each other. But it does not necessarily mean that the message that we want to convey is received in the way we want it to be, because to the Chinese the same word can have a different or a hidden meaning depending on the way or the context in which it is said. There is so much more behind and beyond the language. It is culture at large, with its hidden and sometime mysterious and non-verbal codes, which are very difficult for a foreigner to understand.

Since people from different cultures do not communicate in the same way while speaking together in a common language, it is essential to understand these verbal and non-verbal codes, as well as the importance that the context has on the way people communicate, in order to avoid, or at least reduce to a minimum, the risk of misunderstandings, ambiguity, and confusion that can be very detrimental to the conduct of a business.

5.1. A "high-context" communication style

Edward T. Hall, a 20th century American anthropologist who has written a seminal body of research on cross-cultural communication, has introduced the concepts of "high-context" and "low-context" communication to describe differences between different cultures' communication styles. In his famous book *Beyond Culture* he proposes the following definition for this categorization: "A high-context communication or message is one in which most of the information is either in the physical context or internalized in the person, while very little is in the coded, explicit, transmitted part of the message. A low-context communication is just the opposite; i.e., the mass of the information is vested in the explicit code."[1] China is not only a high-context culture; it is a paradigmatic example of this specific cultural category.

Low-context cultures are more individualistic and task-oriented and focus on explicit verbal communication, while high-context cultures are more collectivistic and relationship-based and focus more on the way and the context in which the message is transmitted rather than on the content itself. To put it simply, in low-context cultures what matters is what is being said, while in high-context cultures what is important is what has not been said.

In terms of communication style, people from low-context cultures (the more low-context in the West being the English-speaking and the German-speaking countries) tend to prefer a direct, linear, and straightforward way of communicating. In high-context cultures such as China, on the contrary, the communication style is indirect and ambiguous (at least for non-Chinese cultural standards) and being too direct is often considered rude and even lacking in sophistication and intelligence. According to a Chinese saying, only the devil walks in a straight line.

Therefore, any businessman who is about to do business in China or to deal with Chinese companies in the West needs to bear in mind this aspect if he wants to engage in a productive communication exchange and reduce the room for ambiguity and misunderstandings. On the one hand, a communication style that is too direct would make the Chinese feel uncomfortable. On the other hand, it is essential to have someone (such as a local advisor or translator) who is able to make sense of the many non-verbal codes and implicit messages that are typical of the Chinese communication style. It is important never to forget that in China there is always more to the message than just the words; to make sense of the real meaning behind what is being said in a meeting, it is essential to pay attention to the wider context and to be able to "read between the lines".

The perceptions many Westerners have is that the Chinese are not straightforward and tend to be vague, ambiguous, and like to beat around the bush. For Western standards it is certainly true, but it is important to understand the reasons behind this attitude in order to enhance the understanding of Chinese culture and reduce the misunderstandings and inconveniences that can hamper effective business communication.

One of the reasons for this has to do with the Chinese language. First, in Mandarin many words can assume a different meaning depending on the context; also, the same word can have different meanings depending on the tone with which it is pronounced. Second, many Western or English words and terms do not necessarily have a direct and clear-cut translation and can be open to different interpretations, and some Mandarin words simply are not as specific as their Western equivalents. This is why in China the explicit and verbal message is vague, and it is only part of the whole message, which can be fully understood only by taking into consideration the social and relational context. Many times Westerners assume that the lack of detail is deliberate; however, in China it is important to have a clear understanding of context and allow for the tendency of language to be vague.[2]

Another reason is more cultural and is related to the importance of harmony and face. As we have seen in previous chapters, in order to preserve harmony it is essential to avoid conflict and confrontation that could disrupt social balance and hierarchy. To achieve this, Confucius himself advocated self-restraint and indirect expression of disapproval by subduing strong feelings in public. In a more modern view of harmony, people should express those strong feelings in a moderate manner according to the concept of *hanxu* (含蓄), which refers to a communicative mode that is contained, reserved, implicit, and indirect.[3]

This is why, most of the time, when the Chinese speak they are indirect in expressing their intentions, and if they want to know something, they usually do not ask it in a straightforward manner. While many Westerners value clarity and a clear communication style, Chinese are much more comfortable with ambiguity.

Actually, it is precisely in the realm of communication that we can really see all the major values of Chinese culture come together into play, posing a major challenge for people coming from cultures that are very different from the Chinese one.

As China is a collectivistic and relationship-based society where *guanxi* plays a central role because of the mistrust they have towards those who are not part of their "in-group", the Chinese are taught from a very early age to hide their true intention behind their words as a form of self-protection. This is why they actually use two types of language: an informal one in the context where there is a high degree of trust, like the family or the circle of close friends, and then a more formal and indirect one for the other situations.[4]

This is why, before being able to develop a good level of *guanxi* with them, the Chinese will not open up in a way that allows the communication exchange to go with the flow and create the opportunity to communicate in a less codified and ritualized way. Therefore, it is very important to remember that, especially at the early stage of any kind of business and working relationship, the Chinese do not go "straight to the point" and do not appreciate people who do. It is only when they have developed a sufficient level of trust that they will feel more comfortable in revealing more of their true intentions and thoughts in a more direct way.

For the sake of preserving the harmony of the group, Chinese are taught from childhood to avoid direct and blunt communication that could lead to a loss of face and to open confrontation. In fact, in the communication process Chinese people are expected to safeguard others by saving face and maintaining social harmony. This is why it is important to convey a message implicitly and indirectly, especially if bad news is being delivered.

5.2. Modesty and humility

Many Westerners used to doing business in informal ways and with not too much consideration for rituals or hierarchies, are often puzzled by how deferential and formal the Chinese can be. What is even more puzzling to them is the way the Chinese can be modest and humble about themselves and, at the same time, praise other people with many compliments.

Humility is actually a very important characteristic of Chinese culture that can be quite difficult to understand especially for Westerners coming from countries (such as the United States) where the showing off of one's accomplishments and successes is accepted and even encouraged. This is why many Americans find it difficult to do business in China, where it is important to demonstrate restraint when it comes to describing one's own strengths or achievements, because the Chinese think that the nobler way to behave is to understate one's accomplishments and let others find ways to identify them.[5]

The importance of humility in Chinese culture can be seen at play very well in the way people react to compliments, because the Chinese tend to debase themselves when someone praises them. This is a very important point that needs to be made when it comes to communication and the misunderstandings that could arise because of a lack of knowledge of the specific cultural codes of the Chinese communication style.

When a Chinese person is complemented she will never respond with a "Thank you!", but will rather debase herself by saying something that indicates that the complement is actually undeserved. Most Chinese will actually respond by saying *Nali Nali*, which literally means "where" but indicates that they think that they are being overpraised. If in most Western cultures it is the acceptance of a compliment that shows respect to the counterpart, in China this respect for the interlocutors is shown through self-deprecation and self-abasement.[6]

Therefore, it is important for any foreign businessman or manager working in China to pay attention to this factor and avoid saying "Thank you" when being praised, which will happen very often because it is a way for the Chinese to give face to their foreign guest. Just saying "Thank you" can be perceived as arrogant and it would not be a good way to start a relationship.

5.3. Yes and No.

Maybe one of the most frustrating situations that any foreigner in China will experience is the fact that most Chinese rarely respond with a direct "yes" or "no" to a question or proposal and tend to use more indirect and vague messages.

The first reason is very simply that, actually, the Chinese language does not really have an exact equivalent for "yes" and "no". If you look in a dictionary for a translation of "yes", for example, the ideograms that you find do not correspond exactly to our affirmative "yes" such as *shi* (是, to be) or *dui* (对, correct). And when you look for the translation of "no" you actually find the same ideograms but preceded by the negation *bu* (不): *bu shi* (不是, it is not) and *bu dui* (不对, not correct). Another reason strictly interwoven with the first one has to do with the holistic and paradoxical character of Chinese thought. As we have seen, the Chinese see contradictions as a positive combination of apparently opposite poles that represent a bigger whole. According to this logic, while for the Western logical mind it is inconceivable that something can be at the same time *yes* and *no*, for the Chinese, imbued by the culture of *Yin* and *Yang*, it is not necessarily true.[7]

Given the high-context character of the Chinese culture, the words are just one part of the picture. As we have seen, non-verbal codes are also of the utmost importance and cannot be neglected. At the beginning of my experience in China, I was making a presentation for a client to a group of potential Chinese investors, and the more I spoke the more confident I was because my interlocutors were nodding to everything I was saying. By seeing their reaction, I was sure that they liked what I was saying and that I would end up doing business with them. But I never heard from them again. The fact is that in China, most of the time when people nod it only means that they understand the meaning of what is being said or that they are listening; it does not necessarily mean that they like what they hear or that they agree with it. This is why it is always very important to pay attention to the many non-verbal cultural codes that make up the Chinese communication style.

But, regardless of what the linguistic and cultural explanations can be, the real tricky issue for many foreigners, especially if they come from very low-context and individualistic cultures, is that the Chinese rarely say a clear and direct "no", because a blunt negative response to an answer or a proposal has the potential to affect the harmony of the group and therefore lead to a loss of face. Therefore, it can happen that if after a first meeting with a foreign counterpart the Chinese are not interested in pursuing the discussion, they will never say that they do not consider the deal or the business interesting for them, but they will rather say that they need to have more internal discussions about it or that they first need to bring the matter to their superiors.

The problem, though, is made even trickier by the fact that if they say so it does not necessarily mean a polite and respectful "no". Many times they actually really need to have more internal discussions before making a decision. It happened to me once many months after a first meeting with a Chinese company when I was told that the management needed some time to consider the business on the table. I was starting to lose hope, and after having opened other negotiations with other companies, the general manager gave me a call and told me that they were ready to move on. This example shows why, in China, it is very important to be patient and flexible when it comes to deciphering what the Chinese really mean. In these situations it is very important to rely on a local intermediary or advisor to monitor informally the development of the situation.

Another point that is important to make is that the Chinese use indirect ways to say "yes" or "no" because many situations are still not clear enough to warrant a definitive and clear answer. For example, saying yes to a proposal without considering the wider context and then not being able, for whatever reason, to follow through would lead to a loss of face. What is certain is that forcing a Chinese person to give a straight answer that he is not ready to give will lead nowhere. In those cases, it is always better to let it go and then come back to it on another occasion, preferably an informal one, and after having established a good working atmosphere.

More generally, any foreigner working or doing business in China should take care to adapt his style of communication, even if it goes against his natural tendencies. One might find it difficult to be too indirect, but there is no shortcut if the goal is to develop a good working relationship with one's Chinese colleagues, employees or partners. At least in the early stages of the relationship, it is really important to avoid any situation that could result, even inadvertently, in a loss of face.

For example, if a Chinese counterpart, colleague or employee says something that is not clear, instead of saying "I didn't understand" or "could you please be clearer", more indirect expressions should be used such as "you said that….as I understand you mean that… Am I correct?".

In the context of a management/employee relationship, it is also very important to try to avoid being too direct in order to preserve the harmony of the relationship. For instance, if an employee did not complete an assignment in the way that was expected by the manager, besides the golden rule of talking to him privately and not in front of the team, unless it is a really serious mistake it can be useful sometimes to take a small part of the blame by saying things such as "maybe my instructions were not very clear, but…" or "maybe I didn't' express myself clearly enough, but…".

Also, if something is not clear, a good way to extract more clarifications and information is to ask the Chinese counterpart/employee for his advice and assistance in reaching a better understanding of a specific situation. In this way, in addition to being able to clarify what is needed, the Chinese interlocutor will gain face and feel useful and important.

5.4. Be clear and do not joke around!

When dealing with the Chinese, even with those who can speak English or another foreign language quite well, in order to reduce the room for potential misunderstandings and confusion (which will always arise anyhow), it is important to use very neat and plain language. Anything more than what is necessary to state a point might actually turn into a pitfall.

There are some linguistic subtleties and expressions that, while being very clear to a foreigner, could be easily misunderstood by the Chinese. For example, expressions like "I couldn't agree more" could be mistaken for "I don't agree". It is really important, every time that one needs to prepare a speech or a presentation, to be as simple and clear as possible by thoroughly reviewing the points that could be a source of misunderstandings.

Another very important rule to follow when it comes to communicating with the Chinese is that one must be very careful with using irony, a rhetorical device that is based on ambiguity (because what is said means actually the opposite) and that is not part of the average Chinese mindset. If you use irony in China, there is a 99 percent probability that what is said in a ironic way will be taken at face value and mistaken for criticism, with the risk of making the interlocutor lose face.

Using humour can also be dangerous. Any culture laughs in different ways at different things, and what is funny to the French is not necessarily funny to an American. And, definitely, what is funny to a Westerner is not necessarily funny to a Chinese person. Generally speaking, few Asians are amused by most Western jokes and, as Richard Lewis has pointed out, "the Confucian and Buddhist preoccupation with truth, sincerity, kindliness and politeness automatically eliminates humour techniques such as sarcasm, satire, exaggeration and parody"[8].

I remember that one day my assistant came into my office all excited because she had just received a call from the assistant of the CEO of a Chinese company we were trying to do business with, who said that her boss was ready to sign a contract. Since I had learned very well that it was good not to believe anything until it was proven true, I told my assistant to calm down and to reserve that excitement for the moment where we would actually see the signature on the contract. As a person who is used to using irony as part of daily communication, I told her that one never knows what could happen that could make the guy change his mind; what if he has a fight with his wife and he sleeps on the sofa and gets up angry and nervous? I was simply trying to make a point, but my assistant started asking questions about what was wrong with the CEO's wife and why had they fought, and how could this have an impact on the company's business, and we got totally lost in a completely surreal conversation. I tried to explain to her that it was a joke, but she could not get it. Not because it was a bad one. She just could not understand that it could be a joke in the first place. Incidentally, that contract has never been signed.

It is therefore important to understand whether the level of the relationship with the person allows for using humour and – most of all – if there is a chance that the joke can be understood for what it is, which can usually only happen with Chinese who have lived for a long time abroad or who have had extensive experience in working closely with Westerners. Even in this case, the context is very important. As a normal rule, it is important not to make jokes in a serious and formal situation like a business meeting, especially if the relationship with the counterpart is in its early stages.

What makes things even more complicated is that, while most Chinese will risk taking messages that are ironic or sarcastic at face value, they may well also start smiling or even laughing in very serious situations where there is nothing to smile or laugh about. This is because Chinese tend to smile or to laugh in difficult situations not to express joy, but to hide their embarrassment, especially when they are about to lose face.

In general, when living and working in China, these are typically the kind of misunderstandings that will definitely arise. Another point that is important to mention is the different concept of politeness that Chinese and Westerners have. While in the West, at least among people who are well mannered, it is good to always say "Please" and "Thank you" otherwise one would be considered rude, in China it is almost the other way around. Saying "thank you" (*xie xie*, 谢谢) is actually a way to establish a level of social distance, which means that among friends it would be considered weird if not rude to thank each other. As a young Chinese person has put it: "Good friends are so close, they are like part of you; why would you say please or thank you to yourself? It doesn't make sense."[9]

By now it is clear that in China misunderstandings and awkward situations are always waiting around the corner and that the process of adaptation to the Chinese communication style can be very long and at times quite frustrating. Every foreigner working in China has experienced some very annoying and confusing situation due to cultural misunderstanding. It is therefore important to be patient, open-minded and a good diplomat to create a dynamic that allows for effective communication with the Chinese. Even more important if a company really wants to support and help its managers through this process is to have a trusted Chinese advisor, assistant or translator as well as a cross-cultural consultant able to act as a "cultural bridge builder" and narrow the communication gaps that, in some cases, can really make or break a business.

SUMMARY

- The Chinese communication style is indirect and ambiguous and being too direct is considered rude.
- To make sense of the real meaning behind what is being said it is essential to be able to "read between the lines".
- While Westerners value clarity and a clear communication style, Chinese are much more comfortable with ambiguity.
- At the beginning of a business relationship Chinese do not go "straight to the point" and do not appreciate people who do it.
- To convey a negative message do it in an implicit and indirect way.
- When receiving a compliment, do not say "Thank you" but say something self-deprecating.
- The Chinese use indirect ways to say "yes" or "no" because many situations are still not clear enough to call for a definitive and clear answer.
- Try to avoid asking "closed" questions that require a "yes" or "no" answer.
- Never force a Chinese to give a straight answer that he is not ready to give.
- Always use a very neat and simple language.
- Avoid using humour or sarcasm, which could lead to misunderstandings.
- Often Chinese smile or laugh not to express joy, but to hide their embarrassment, especially if they are about to lose face.

1 Hall, Edward T., *Beyond Culture*, Anchor Books, New York, 1989, p. 91.

2 Upton-McLaughlin, Sean, « Tips For Communicating With The Chinese, Part 1, https://chinaculturecorner.com/2013/09/24/how-to-communicate-with-the-chinese-part-1/.

3 Wei, Xiaohong & Li, Qingyuan, « The Confucian Value of Harmony and its Influence on Chinese Social Interaction », in Cross-Cultural Communication, Vol. 9, No. 1, 2013, p. 63.

4 Zhang, Haihua & Baker, Geoff, *Think Like Chinese*, The Federation Press, Annandale, 2013, p. 83.

5 Wee, Chow-Hou & Combe, Fred, *Business Journey to the East. An East-West Perspective on Global-is-Asian*, McGraw-Hill, Singapore, 2009, p. 261.

6 Zhu, Jiang & Bao, Yuxiao, « The Pragmatic Comparison of Chinese and Western Politeness in Cross-cultural Communication », in *Journal of Language Teaching and Research*, Vol. 1, No. 6, November 2010, p. 850.

7 Javary, Cyrille J.-D., *La souplesse du dragon. Les fondamentaux de la culture chinoise*, Albin Michel, Paris, 2014, p. 138.

8 Lewis, Richard D., *When Cultures Collide. Leading across cultures*, Nicholas Brealey International, Boston-London, 2006.

[9] Fallows, Deborah, « How Thank You Sounds to Chinese Ears »,
The Atlantic, 12.6.2015,
http://www.theatlantic.com/international/archive/2015/06/thank
-you-chinese/395660/.

6

NEGOTIATION

For any company doing business across borders and cultures, developing a good level of cultural intelligence is essential, especially when it comes to negotiations. If negotiations can be sometimes challenging even with people coming from similar cultural perspectives, the task becomes particularly difficult, and at times even daunting, when dealing with people with a completely different cultural background. In these cases, a lack of cultural intelligence could compromise the business regardless of the intrinsic value of the deal at hand.

Culture influences people's behaviour, mindset and attitude and it is therefore an important variable that has a critical impact on international negotiations. This impact assumes a particular significance in the context of negotiations with Chinese companies, because the Chinese negotiation processes and style are shaped by very specific cultural traits that it would be irresponsible to neglect or even to underestimate.

Many companies that have tried to enter the Chinese market have failed because they were not prepared to aptly adapt their negotiation strategies and tactics to the Chinese business battlefield. Often, not only their managers were not adequately trained to face a team of Chinese negotiators with their very specific negotiation style, but they did not even take into serious consideration the fact that in China there is more than a different way of negotiating; the real issue is that in China the overall meaning of negotiation itself takes a whole different dimension. In fact, whereas the Western negotiation concept is to create a onetime agreement between two parties, the Chinese view negotiation as a process for creating a framework for long-term cooperation. As we have seen before, in China relationships come before business, which means that, without an effort in establishing a good level of *guanxi*, negotiations rarely lead to the expected result and can be a very long and frustrating experience.

6.1. The Chinese negotiator

The backbone of Chinese business culture is still shaped by the long historical and cultural heritage of Chinese civilization. Consequently, the Chinese negotiation style is influenced by different Chinese cultural traits such as: Confucianism, the holistic perspective of the world, the *Yin Yang* mindset, and the Chinese inclination for strategic thought epitomized by historical texts such as the *The Art of War* or the *36 Stratagems*, a compendium of deceptive tactics aimed at winning the battle with the adversary without directly fighting them on the battlefield. This is actually the principle that is at the core of Chinese strategic thought and that was summarized by Sun

Tzu, the author of *The Art of War*, in the following way: "To win one hundred victories in one hundred battles is not the acme of skill. To subdue the enemy without fighting is the acme of skill."[1]

What the Chinese call stratagems include means such as concealment, deception, and espionage aimed at exhausting, destabilizing, and weakening the adversary. After centuries of practicing them in the context of warfare and imperial politics, they have come to shape the Chinese mindset and we can still see them at play in modern business negotiations. In fact, the Chinese proverb "The marketplace is a battlefield" reflects a deep-seated belief that the wisdom that guides the general commander in the battlefield is the same one that applies to business.[2]

In the last few decades of China's economic boom, countless Western businessmen have learned just how shrewd, clever, and even manipulative Chinese negotiators can be. From their perspective, it is easy to understand that these tactics, more than stratagems, are seen as pure and simply "dirty tricks". But it is important to understand that, while Westerners see deception as evil because they perceive their ethical norms to be universally applicable, in China, where ethical duties are not absolute but dependent on a specific context and situation, the motives for deception can be virtuous. In fact, having been influenced by centuries of strategic thought based on the teachings of Sun Tzu, the Chinese regard the use of stratagems for handling hostile opponents or outsiders as ethical behaviour.[3] This last point is actually very important, because Chinese negotiators are not manipulative *per se*, but will adapt their negotiating style depending on their degree of trust of their counterpart.

According to Tony Fang, a scholar who has been studying the Chinese negotiation style for decades, there are two main types of Chinese negotiators: the "Confucian gentleman" and the "Sun Tzu-like strategist". The first one behaves on the basis of mutual trust and benefit, seeking cooperation and "win-win" solutions for everybody to succeed. He is reluctant to involve lawyers in face-to-face discussions and views contracting as an ongoing relationship or problem-solving process rather than a one-off legal package. He can be a daunting negotiator when he revisits old issues in the light of a new market situation to seek mutual benefits for both parties, and his negotiation strategy is characterized basically by *cooperation*.[4] On the other hand, the "Sun Tzu-like strategist" sees negotiation as a zero-sum game and the marketplace as a battlefield. He never stops bargaining and is keen on a psychological wrestling of wit to manipulate his counterpart into doing business his way. His actions tend to be deceitful and indirect and his negotiation strategy is characterized by *competition*.[5]

These are the two main profiles of the Chinese negotiators that can be found in any situation, but there is a third one that is more specifically related to state-owned companies or to corporations whose business is strictly linked to government strategies and authority. He is what Tony Fang has called a "Maoist bureaucrat" and he might be the most difficult to deal with, especially from a Western perspective. This negotiator has only one agenda, and it is the one set by the government. He gives first priority to China's national interest and never separates business from politics. He avoids taking initiatives, shuns responsibility, fears criticism and has no final say. He is a shrewd and tough negotiator because he is trained daily in Chinese bureaucracy in which bargaining is an integrated element. He is the most elusive and inscrutable negotiator because of the changing nature of the Chinese government's policies, strategies, and priorities.[6]

Given the pragmatic, holistic, and synthetic character of Chinese culture, the Chinese negotiator is obviously more complex than a schematic categorization between a cooperative or competitive style of negotiation. Depending on the context, he can use both cooperation and competition, and combine them in a strategic mix. This is why the Chinese negotiation style can appear at times contradictory and inscrutable: the Confucian tradition and the Chinese stratagems have bestowed on the Chinese what Tony Fang has described as a culturally embedded "coop-comp" strategy with which to negotiate both sincerely and deceptively.[7]

Eventually, the negotiation style adopted by the Chinese will be influenced by the attitude of their counterpart and by the level of trust that both parties will be able to establish. If a foreign businessman does not take the time to build trust, he will face a ruthless Chinese negotiator; if he understands the importance of *guanxi*, he will meet a much more cooperative one. Certainly, regardless of the negotiating style adopted by the Chinese, in China no negotiation will ever be easy for anyone. Any company willing to do business in the Chinese market needs to prepare better than usual for the negotiation and be prepared for many unexpected twists and turns. But whether and how foreign negotiators will be able to master these twists and turns and eventually reach a satisfactory deal will depend very much on their attitude and their ability to adapt to the local context by understanding that building good personal relationships with the Chinese is the first essential step towards building a successful business.

6.2. Pre-negotiation: building trust and guanxi

The pre-negotiation phase is essential in China more than anywhere else, because it is then that a foreign business person has the opportunity to create the right conditions and relational frameworks that will come in handy later on when problems and disagreements arise, because they always do. In this context, the two golden rules to follow are always the same and it is never redundant to reiterate them.

First, in China relationships come before business and not the other way around. This means that, before rushing into

119

the details of a deal, the Chinese want first to build a personal relationship and create an adequate level of trust between the parties. I have seen many foreign entrepreneurs go to China to meet their counterpart for the first time, with the expectation of getting at least a commitment to move forward or even to have some kind of formal document signed. But this usually does not happen. Even if the general framework of the potential business deal has been prepared through a local advisor, and the potential counterpart has expressed interest in discussing it, it is not enough. Before moving forward, the Chinese want to have the time to establish a personal connection with their direct counterpart.

From this ensues the second golden rule of doing business in China: the Chinese do not do business with your company, but with you. Therefore, even if the Chinese counterpart has developed a good working and personal relationship with the local advisor of the foreign company, it is with the company's leaders that they will do business and it is with them that a relationship needs to be built.

Building a personal relationship based on mutual trust takes time anywhere, but in China it takes much longer, especially for someone coming from abroad. According to the famous theory on trust developed by American political scientist Francis Fukuyama[8], China is actually considered a low-trust society, where people tend to trust only the members of their social circle, their "in-group", while distrusting the "strangers" who are not part of it. This means that the Chinese are naturally and intrinsically suspicious of their "out-groups", and nobody is more "out-group" than a foreigner.

Therefore, a foreigner, even more than a Chinese stranger, must go a long way to show that he can be trusted. Sometimes, for example, doing a personal favour that is completely unrelated with the business at hand can produce amazing results. I have heard stories of foreign businessmen who, in one shot, managed to become part of some influential *guanxi* and open business opportunities out of the range of their competitors, simply by finding a good school abroad for the kids of their Chinese counterpart. This is why, when doing initial due diligence on a potential Chinese partner, it could be useful for a foreign business person to check informally through some local advisor or intermediary to see whether there is a way to do the potential Chinese partner a favour in some way, because that would certainly smooth things out and change the dynamics of the business relationship by turning it into a more personal one. In most cases, though, there is no such opportunity, and for a foreigner it is therefore essential to be patient and take the time to let his Chinese counterpart get to know him and build a personal connection.

Against this cultural background, it is clear that foreign managers and business people who are used to getting things done quickly and efficiently because "time is money" need to reset their mindset because in China haste simply does not work. One of the most frustrating things for those foreign business people who go to China without having been properly prepared is to find out that the first meeting with a Chinese counterpart is usually not (or never) as business-oriented as most Westerners – especially the English-speaking Westerners – are used to. These meetings seem very inconsequential and full of vague words about "friendship" and "cooperation" to most foreign businessmen who like to get straight to the point. But as China is a "high context" culture, most Chinese consider going straight to the point during a first meeting rude and lacking in sophistication. To them, this first encounter represents only the beginning of a trust-building process. Attempting to force their hand because you need to catch your flight back home will not lead you very far.

Generally speaking, someone who is expecting a concrete result after a first meeting in China will likely be disappointed and frustrated. Most of the time, the Chinese will close the first meeting by saying that they will "have internal discussions about it…" or that they will "have to introduce the deal to the board" before making a further step. Sometimes it will be a polite way to say that they are not interested, because saying it in a blunt way would make their counterpart lose face. But sometimes it can really mean that, while they are interested, they need to follow the proper internal decision processes before making a decision on whether to go forward or not.

In any case, if one is really serious about doing business in China, it is essential to take the time to follow up on the first meeting by going back to China more than once in order to establish a relationship with the counterpart, especially outside of the business setting. Participating in social events is actually essential to building a personal connection. The Chinese are very good and generous hosts and take pride and pleasure in inviting foreigners for dinner or for social activities. It is not just about business. They really want to get to know their counterpart as a person first. Therefore, it is always very important to accept any invitation. Declining it is seen as an insult that will make them lose face and could actually affect the whole business. Besides, a very good way to build a relationship is to invite the Chinese to visit your country and your company and reciprocate with as much hospitality and generosity.

It is also very important to "give face" to the Chinese, for example by inviting them for dinner, by giving gifts, and by showing interest in their family and their culture. Actually, knowing even just a little bit about Chinese culture and history is a very good way to show them that there is a genuine interest in establishing a long-term relationship with them based on friendship and trust. Not rushing into the details of the potential deal, and taking the time to create a genuine personal connection with the counterpart by taking part in non business-related activities will come to help when problems or tensions arise during the negotiation process. Thus preventing the Chinese negotiators from resorting to the deceitful stratagems typical of the "Sun Tzu-like strategist".

6.3. The three "P"s for negotiation: patience, patience, patience

When preparing for a negotiation in China, the choice of the right negotiating team is essential. Normally, Chinese companies send a big group of people to the business meetings, and often outnumber the foreign delegations. When possible, sending a big delegation conveys status and importance, and gives you face in front of your counterpart; the bigger the better.

However, not all companies (especially SMEs) can afford to send as many people as the Chinese counterparts do, so it is essential to focus on quality and send the right negotiators. Besides the technical managers or consultants who will have to answer the many technical and financial questions raised by the Chinese, it is important that the delegation be led by a chief negotiator who has the profile of a "corporate diplomat", meaning someone who has the right "soft" skills and the cultural intelligence to engage in a productive way with the Chinese counterpart. A manager who is not known for his open mind, who is not intellectually flexible, who is not curious about other cultures, and who perhaps has a smug attitude towards the Chinese and shows no interest in their food, might not be the ideal fit.

It is also very important to consider that, since the Chinese value experience and seniority, too young a manager, no matter how competent and brilliant, might not be taken as seriously as an older one. Most importantly, given the value that the Chinese put on hierarchy, it is essential to know the hierarchical position of the Chinese counterpart, and send managers to China who are at a corresponding hierarchical level. If the Chinese team is led by the CEO of the company, sending a manager with a lower rank would be seen as a serious offense and insult.

Once the negotiating team has been chosen, it is very important not to change it along the way, especially the chief negotiator. Since the Chinese do not do business with an organization but with its people, if they have established a good relationship with a specific person, his successor will not automatically inherit his *guanxi* and this could be an issue affecting the negotiation process.

When it comes to the style of negotiations in China, the "soft" skills of the corporate diplomat are essential and the lack thereof can have "hard" consequences. Generally speaking, in a business meeting in China there is a high need for harmony, and care should be taken to preserve good will and avoid unnecessary tension. It is true that the first meetings with their vague and ritual formulas coupled with the indirect and "high-context" communication style of the Chinese can be very annoying and frustrating to many Westerners. But it is absolutely essential to hold back and to control emotions because an open display of anger, irritability, frustration or aggression at the negotiating table will cause both parties to lose face and can be disastrous to negotiations.

If there is an important and critical point that needs to be discussed, it is really important not to raise it in a blunt way, but to use a more indirect form of communication and politely ask the Chinese counterpart for their opinion and advice on how to deal with the matter. It is a way to avoid a direct confrontation while giving face to the Chinese interlocutor. Also, if the discussion gets jammed by a contentious issue, instead of insisting and forcing the hand of the Chinese counterpart, it is better to show patience, and therefore respect, and propose to look at the matter later and focus on other points. In these cases, a good option would be to wait for more informal situations to raise unresolved issues, like a dinner or around some drinks when the atmosphere is more relaxed.

During the discussions, the Chinese usually speak with only one voice through a "spokesperson" and respect the hierarchy in terms of whom can or cannot speak and when. The foreign team should act accordingly with the chief negotiator leading the discussion and giving the word to another member of the team when necessary, for example when special technical expertise is required to answer some questions that the counterpart might have. It is also very important to show a strong cohesiveness within the team and absolutely not show possible tensions or disagreements as it would show weakness.

When meeting with a Chinese counterpart, small talk is an essential part of the game and it would be a shame to spoil the atmosphere by bringing up topics that could create embarrassment or even offense. For example, it is absolutely forbidden to bring up taboo topics such as Tibet, Taiwan or the human rights situation in China. Instead, it is always a good thing to ask questions about family and children and to give face to the Chinese hosts by praising the amazing accomplishments made by China in the last few decades and by showing interest and curiosity about their history, culture, and food.

As for the structure of negotiations, Westerners must be prepared for a whole new context that is shaped by the deeply different conception that Chinese have of time. According to Edward T. Hall, the Chinese have a polychronic attitude towards time, which means that for them time is cyclical like the seasons of nature. On the other hand, Westerners are monochronic, meaning that they see time as linear, inflexible, and sequential. This is why for many Westerners time is money, and a fixed and precise schedule almost sacred.[9] Asian negotiators, on the other hand, have a greater facility with a messy and less structured agenda, and they can easily move cyclically between issues and handle multiple issues in parallel.[10]

Furthermore, being shaped by a linear, logical, and

analytical mindset, most Westerners like to break things down into individual elements and look at them one at a time while the Chinese – given their holistic perspective on things – will jump from one subject to the other and talk about everything all at once. To the Chinese, the different details of a project cannot be separated into single entities, but must be seen as part of something bigger. At first it is important to reach an agreement on the general objectives of the deal without being obsessed by the single items of the potential deal. This is why the opening statement of the foreign company (which, by the way, should also be translated into Chinese and given to the counterpart) should focus on the general objectives of the business that must be framed within the context of a long-term commitment towards the Chinese market and the advantages that the foreign technology or know-how can bring to China's development.

Since the negotiations start with the general principles and then move to the details, it is important not to force the Chinese's hand by trying to rush from general to specific.[11] At the early stage of a negotiation, in the process leading to the signature of a Memorandum of Understanding or a Letter of Intent, many foreign companies tend to fill the documents with too many details and the Chinese are often put off and stall. Most importantly, putting too much focus on legal provisions and binding documents at the early stage of the negotiation might be perceived by the Chinese as a lack of trust in them and therefore undermine the process of relationship building.

Furthermore, the Chinese know very well how time and deadlines are important to foreign businessmen and they can easily play with that and take advantage of their counterpart's need to proceed fast. They know that businessmen who have travelled across the world hope to go back home with some concrete results, and therefore they have learned that exerting pressure on foreigners just before they fly home can often create useful benefits for them. What can easily happen is that they agree on all the easy items of the deal and leave the most difficult ones for the end, hoping to use the time pressure to lead the foreign counterpart to concede in order to avoid leaving China empty-handed.[12]

It is therefore very important to be very patient and not to disclose to the Chinese your own timetable and deadlines. Even when the Chinese have themselves an interest in speeding up the process, they will always project an attitude of not being in a hurry, because they understand the strategic value of time and are mindful of controlling the pace of the negotiation.[13]

Patience is really the most important asset one needs to have when negotiating with the Chinese. Fast and smooth negotiations in China, if they ever happen, are most definitely the exception to the rule. Anyone who is starting a negotiation with a Chinese company must be prepared for a long process that can wear down even the most skilled and experienced negotiator. Sometimes carrying out long negotiations can certainly be a tactic to extract concessions when getting closer to the deal, but many times the reason for protracted negotiations is due to the decision making process within Chinese companies, especially if they are state-owned or indirectly linked with the government.

Often the real decision-makers are not even in the negotiating room until the very end of the process, and their subordinates do not want and cannot take personal responsibility and therefore go back and forth to consult with their bosses. This is why it is very important to understand from the outset, through one's local advisor or through other informal channels, who the real decision-makers are and try to establish direct communication with them in order to understand whether they are really interested in the business or they are simply trying to extract information without any real commitment.

As anyone who has done business in China knows very well, the Chinese are very price-conscious and can be very hard and effective bargainers. It is therefore essential for any foreign company preparing for a negotiation with a Chinese counterpart to include in their strategy from the outset a clear framework allowing for a flexible and effective haggling process that can preserve both the company's interest and the counterpart's face.

When preparing to negotiate prices with a Chinese company, it is essential to bear in mind two important facts. On the one hand, if the foreign company reduces its price too much the Chinese counterpart might get suspicious and the foreigners would lose face and, with it, their credibility. On the other hand, if the foreign company did not build a flexible margin for negotiation and refuses any price reduction, the Chinese would most likely feel insulted.[14] It is therefore very important for a foreign company to always add a buffer to its price that allows for a price reduction, which will show both goodwill and help the Chinese negotiators gain face.

More generally, it is always important to leave sufficient room for concessions at many different levels and prepare several alternative options, because for the Chinese conceding something is part of the "face giving" and trust building process necessary to create a genuine relationship between partners. This is why if a foreign company makes concessions, the Chinese side is expected to reciprocate. However, it is important not to make significant concessions in the early stages of the negotiation, because the Chinese will certainly try to extract further concessions along the way.

Generally speaking, Western negotiators tend to reduce a complex negotiation problem into several parts or issues, discuss them one at a time and then settle each before moving on to the next one. This means that concessions are made throughout the negotiation process and somehow the final agreement is a sequence of smaller agreements. But the Chinese do not work this way. They see negotiation with a holistic perspective; their approach is to discuss all issues at once without apparent focus or order, and concessions are made only at the end of the negotiations.[15] This is why they will often settle all suspending items in a "package deal". Therefore, generally speaking, concessions should be given only when an agreement has been reached and when they will serve as symbols of goodwill rather than as bargaining chips; for many Chinese, in fact, final concessions are "face giving", meaning that they demonstrate to other people in their organizations that their negotiations with the foreigners have been successful.[16]

To sum it up, for the Chinese nothing is settled until everything is settled, and they focus more on the whole package than on the details. Therefore, it is important not to invest too many resources and energy on individual details at the outset of the negotiation and to focus instead on the bigger picture.

6.3. Contracts and post-negotiation

When approaching the signature of a deal with a Chinese company, foreigners, especially Westerners, need to be prepared to reset their mindset to face the inevitable twists and turns that negotiating with the Chinese imply. Actually, it is at this stage of the negotiation process where the Chinese business culture (and the Asian culture more generally) differs the most from Western practices. With no cultural adaption and without the necessary flexibility to adjust its actions to the Chinese environment, a foreign company risks getting caught unprepared and losing its focus.

What is really different between the West and China is the role and importance of contracts. While in the West the signing of a contract is seen as the end of the negotiation, in China it is merely an act that states the beginning of a long-term relationship. And, most importantly, while most

Westerners view contracts as a list of legally binding rights and obligations, Chinese see them only as a list of rights and obligations that need to be respected *depending on the situation*. To them a contract starts a long-term commitment between two trusted partners and friends, and they take for granted the fact that it will need to be revisited if the context in which it was signed changes. Being intrinsically pragmatic, the Chinese consider that if the conditions of the market change dramatically, the deal between the two partners must be adapted to the new conditions.

This is why Western contracts usually tend to be quite lengthy and wordy in order to cover every possible contingency with precision, leaving as little ambiguity as possible. Chinese contracts are much less legalistic and therefore their business contracts are often specified in legal terms yet implemented on the basis of personal trust and relationships between the parties involved. Asians in general prefer a vague agreement because it leaves plenty of room for adjustment later if things do not work out as expected, and they dislike the Western process of going through the contract line by line because "it removes the warmth and spirit of the relationship, the sincerity of the partnership, and converts it into a cold, lifeless piece of paper"[17]. For example, many Chinese still feel very uncomfortable about the expression "legally binding", seeing it as a sign of lack of trust, and when push comes to shove the discussion could stall and even stop if a good personal relationship able to offset the legalistic part of the negotiation has not been established.

Within this context, a foreign company needs to be able to play a balancing act between the need to protect its interests (especially when it comes to the protection of intellectual property) and the necessity to play by the Chinese rules in order to establish a trustworthy and genuine relationship with its business partner. Therefore, it is certainly essential to work with good lawyers to protect a company's interests by including the appropriate clauses in the contract, while being flexible and open to renegotiate the deal in suitable terms in order to show goodwill, respect, and trust.

This is why it is really important to have a contingency plan that includes a predetermined method for resolving any dispute that might arise (arbitration, mediation) and a provision specifying eventual damages in case of renegotiation. In any case, the best way of managing conflicts and solving disputes in China is to avoid them. Given the importance of values such as harmony and face, and the historical lack of a legal framework similar to the ones in place in the West, the Chinese tend to use indirect ways to avoid direct and open conflict. If it becomes unavoidable, they prefer to resolve it through negotiation and compromise usually with the help of a "go-between" who is usually part of their *guanxi*.

One of Confucius's teachings to preserve harmony among people was the ideal of a "no litigation" society. Still today, resolving disputes by going to a court of justice is seen in a negative way, because there is a huge potential for both parties involved to lose their face. In the case of foreign companies, it is always best to try to solve a conflict through an informal third party and through negotiation, since going to court in China drags on and does not necessarily lead to the desired outcome. If neither negotiation nor mediation work, it is essential to have a good team of Chinese lawyers and, most of all, to have a clause of arbitration in every contract signed in China.

In conclusion, negotiating with a Chinese company is a long and difficult process that requires cultural dexterity, strategic and tactical flexibility, and a huge amount of patience. In any negotiation with the Chinese, problems, tensions, surprises, and setbacks will most certainly arise; it is simply part of the game. And in order to be able to play the game and win it, it is absolutely essential to turn the legalistic and task-oriented Western perspective into a more China-compatible way of doing business that include a serious and genuine commitment to developing long-term personal relationships with the Chinese. As we have seen, credibility and trust need to be established early in the game. Therefore, priority must be given from the beginning to create the appropriate *relational* framework with the Chinese counterpart. Once trust and friendship are part of the picture, it will be much easier to overcome any problem that might arise and close the deal.

SUMMARY

- In China, the goal of a negotiation is not to create a one-time agreement, but to build long-term cooperation.
- The Chinese adapt their negotiating style depending on their degree of trust with their counterpart.
- If a foreign business person does not take the time to build trust, he will face a ruthless Chinese negotiator; if he understands the importance of *guanxi*, he will meet a much more cooperative one.
- Before rushing into the details of a deal, the Chinese want to build a personal relationship and create an adequate level of trust.
- Having the opportunity to do a personal favour for the Chinese counterpart can help build a *guanxi* and smooth the negotiation process.
- Do not expect concrete results after a first meeting.
- Take the time to participate to business unrelated social activities to build trust and friendship with your counterpart. Never decline an invitation.
- The choice of the right negotiating team is essential. The bigger the team the better. The chief negotiator should be a senior manager. Seniority is very valued in China.
- Rank is very important. If the Chinese team is led by the CEO of the company, sending a manager with a lower rank would be seen as a serious offense and insult.
- Always behave in a calm and respectful way and never show anger, irritability, and frustration.

- Never raise a critical point in a blunt way.
- Always be patient, and never force the hand of your Chinese counterpart.
- Always show cohesiveness. Tensions or disagreements within the team must not be shown.
- Never bring up taboo topics such as Tibet, Taiwan or the human rights situation in China.
- Chinese negotiators are comfortable with unstructured agendas and move easily between issues and handle multiple issues in parallel.
- In China negotiations start with the general principles and then move to the details. It is important not to force the hand of the Chinese by trying to rush from general to specific too soon.
- To the Chinese the details of a project cannot be separated into single entities, but must be seen as parts of something bigger.
- Do not focus too much on wordy and detailed legal provisions and binding documents at the early stage of the negotiation.
- When it comes to price negotiations, include from the outset a clear framework allowing for a flexible and effective haggling process.
- Do not make significant concessions in the early stages of the negotiation.
- In China, the signature of a contract is only the beginning of a long-term relationship.
- Expect demands for renegotiation of the contract.
- Prepare a contingency plan that includes a predetermined method for resolving any dispute that might arise and a provision specifying eventual damages in case of renegotiation.

DECODING CHINA

[1] Quote from : Ghauri, Pervez & Fang, Tony, « Negotiating with the Chinese : A Socio-Cultural Analysis », in *Journal of World Business*, 36.3, Fall 2001, p. 310.

[2] Fang, Tony, « Negotiation : the Chinese style », in *Journal of Business & Industrial Marketing*, 21/1, 2006, p. 53.

[3] Sebenius, James K. & Qiang, Cheng, « Cultural Notes on Chinese Negotiating Behavior », *Harvard Business School*, Working Paper 09-076, December 24, 2008, p. 5.

[4] Fang, *op. cit.*

[5] *Ibid.*

[6] *Ibid.*

[7] *Ibid.*

[8] Fukuyama, Francis, *Trust : The Social Virtues and The Creation of Prosperity*, Free Press Paperbacks, New York, 1996.

[9] Hall, Edward T., *The Silent Language*, Anchor Books, New York, 1973, p. 157.

[10] Benoliel, Michael, « Negotiating Successfully in Asia », in *Eurasian Journal of Social Sciences*, 1(1), 2013, p. 6.

[11] Akgunes, Asuman & Culpepper, Robert, « Negotiations Between Chinese and Americans : Examining the Cultural Context and Salient Factors », in *The Journal of International Management Studies*, Vol. 7, No. 1, April 2012, p. 196.

[12] Wee, Chow-Hou & Combe, Fred, *Business Journey to the East. An*

East-West Perspective on Global-is-Asian, McGraw-Hill, Singapore, 2009, p. 109.

[13] Beloniel, *op. cit.*, p. 12.

[14] Turner, Stephen P., *How to Win in China. Business and Negotiation Strategies Revealed*, L&T Publishing, Austin, 2011, p. 220.

[15] Lee, Kam-hon Lee, Yang, Guang & Graham, John L., "Tension and trust in international business negotiations: American executives negotiating with Chinese executives", in *Journal of International Business Studies*, 37, September 2006, p. 626. |

[16] March, Robert M. & Wu, Su-Hua, *The Chinese Negotiator. How to Succeed in the World's Largest Market*, Kodansha International, Tokyo-New York-London, 2007, p. 230.

[17] Wee & Combe, *op. cit.*, p. 138.

7

七

BUSINESS ETIQUETTE

- Always be on time. Chinese value punctuality.
- Wear formal dress. The Chinese can sometimes wear very informal outfits, and you can feel "overdressed" compared to them; but they expect you to be dressed in a formal "Western" way. In any case, if in doubt, go formal.
- Never throw your business card at people – it is considered very rude. Cards must be presented by holding them with both hands and must be received in the same way. Once you receive a business card from someone, do not put it in your pocket or in your bag; take your time to read it carefully and then do not put it away but lay it out on the table in front of you. It shows respect and

regard for the person. It is always a good thing, in order to create a first good impression, to ask information about the meaning of the Chinese name of the person.

- It is better if your business card has information printed in English on one side and in Chinese on the other. Gold is the best colour to use.

- People must be addressed with their surname, which in China comes before the first name. It is also important to know and use the titles of the people that you will meet. Be sure to know the title beforehand; it is considered very inappropriate to ask for it at the meeting in front of everyone.

- Body posture should always be formal in a way that you convey self-control and respectfulness.

- Never interrupt people while they are speaking.

- Never challenge a person directly.

- If your counterpart seems to be unwilling or unable to give you the information that you requested, do not insist and wait for a better time.

- Never lose your temper and always keep your calm and a respectful and restrained demeanour.

- While speaking, do not use large hand movements.

- Do not point with your index finger, but use an open palm.

- Putting fingers in your mouth, biting your nails or removing food from your mouth is considered very rude.

- If you have to bring up an unpleasant topic with a person, never do so in public and always express your message in a way that preserve the other's "face".

- Never bring up "taboo topics" such as Tibet, Taiwan, or the human rights situation.

- Show genuine interest for Chinese culture and customs and praise China's accomplishments. Showing some knowledge of Chinese history is always a good way to make a first good impression and start on the right foot.
- In a formal meeting, when your Chinese host changes topic and stops discussing business, do not insist on talking business again.
- Do not accept a compliment with a "Thank you", but rather with a "Not at all" or "It's nothing".
- The Chinese have a different concept of privacy. Do not be surprised when asked personal questions about age, family, income, etc.
- In a business lunch or dinner there is a strict hierarchy regarding the seating at the table; do not sit before your host, and if you do not know where to sit ask them for instructions.
- Do not start eating before your host begins.
- During a meal, be prepared to drink a lot of alcohol (the most common being the Chinese liquor *baijiu*). Before drinking, wait for the host to make the first toast (*gan bei*). If your host finishes his glass in one shot, which is often the case, you should do the same. As a guest, you should always stand up and propose a toast to your host and thank him for his hospitality by making a wish for a fruitful and long-term friendship and cooperation.
- Do not drink until you toast others at the table. Chinese consider drinking alone to be rude.
- At the typical Chinese meal there are several courses. As a sign of respect you should sample all the dishes you are offered.

- Do not place your chopsticks upright in your bowl, which symbolizes death, but place them neatly on the table or on the chopstick rest.

- Always leave some food on your plate; it shows that you have eaten enough, which is very important to the Chinese.

- Compliment your Chinese partner for their mastery of English (even when they are not that good).

- Hire a professional translator/interpreter who does not have any interest in the discussion.

- When possible, translate presentations and material into Chinese.

- Avoid direct eye contact and do not stare at people.

- Avoid physical contact with the exception of a handshake, but do not hold the hand too hard and for too long. Do not hug and do not kiss; it can make people feel very uncomfortable.

- If you bring a gift, it is a good thing to bring gifts that symbolize your country, but avoid lavish or expensive ones. Today, after the anti-corruption campaign launched by president Xi Jinping, it is better not to bring gifts to government related companies, but only to private corporations.

- The best colour for the wrapping paper is red, which in China represents success, happiness and good luck. Gold is also good. Avoid black and white, which are the colours of mourning and death.

- Gifts to avoid include items associated with death such as clocks, cut flowers or anything white or black, as well as scissors or other sharp items as they symbolize severing relations.

- When giving or receiving a gift always use both hands.

- When receiving a gift, do not open it right away but wait until after you have left.
- Before planning your schedule, be aware of the major holidays in China, especially Chinese New Year (late January/February) and National Holiday (late September/October).
- Keep in mind that Chinese are very superstitious when it comes to numbers. 6, 8 and 9 are lucky numbers, while 4 and 14 are very unlucky ones.

8

八

CONCLUSION

Doing business in or with China is hard, and it is not for everyone. At first you need to be very patient, very flexible, very open minded and with a thick skin. But this is not enough. Dealing with the Chinese, whether it is in China or abroad, requires a wide set of skills, the most important of which is cultural intelligence.

Too many business people still underestimate the impact of cultural differences when working across different countries and cultures. They see culture as something "soft", but the consequences of neglecting the importance of culture can be very "hard", as many companies have learned at their expense. According to recent studies, up to 70 percent of international ventures fail because of cultural differences.[1]

This is even more true with regards to China. As we have seen throughout this book, the civilizational and philosophical principles that have shaped Chinese culture over more than two millennia continue to influence the way the Chinese think and behave, and therefore the way they work and do business. For this reason it is essential to have a good understanding of

Chinese cultural codes if one wants to deal successfully with the Chinese, whether it is in China or not.

China is changing at a dramatic pace and this change certainly has a major impact not only on the Chinese economy but on Chinese society and Chinese culture as well. But "modernization" does not necessarily rhyme with "Westernization". Very proud and very pragmatic at the same time, China is modernizing in a Chinese way, and it would be a great mistake to think that, simply through the interaction with other cultures coming with the globalization of the economy, Chinese culture will wholly absorb Western cultural codes.

Furthermore, China is more powerful and influential than ever on the global stage, and the young generations are increasingly nationalistic due to pride in China's accomplishments. It is therefore reasonable to expect that cultural differences are not going to ebb away any time soon. In fact, according to recent research on the Hofstede's cultural dimensions mentioned in the second chapter, when cultures change they change in absolute and not relative terms, meaning that in the last decades countries have moved along the same path with value differences between countries staying more or less the same.[2]

It is therefore essential for anyone who is serious about doing business in China, or for anyone who is or will be faced with Chinese business people abroad, to put cultural intelligence at the core of their strategy. This means putting the right resources in place to develop a correct and thorough cultural understanding of the country that goes far beyond the still important yet superficial "dos and don'ts" that are part of many short-term oriented and narrow-in-scope expat training programs.

Moreover, in the case of managers being assigned to a post in China, it is also very important that the executives at HQ be sensitized to how difficult it is to operate in such a different cultural business environment. One of the biggest problems of many companies doing business in China is actually the fact that foreign managers in China often feel that they lack the appropriate support from their HQ and that their insights on how to run the business are not taken into the right consideration by the people back home who have no idea of how important it is to profoundly adapt and adjust strategies and business models to the Chinese market.

As we have said many times, China is changing very fast, but with it the whole world is changing very fast too. Gone is the time when the West, led by the United States, was enjoying almost hegemonic economic and geopolitical power around the world. The unipolar world borne out of the ashes of the Cold War is over. We are now living in an increasingly multipolar world, where new players from the East and the South of the world are redefining the global balance of power. And China is definitely the most important and the most powerful of these players.

Actually, when seen in a broader historical perspective, this is nothing new. From the beginning of our era up until the first quarter of the 19th century, when Europe took off as a global power thanks to the industrial revolution, China and India together accounted for over half of the global economic output. Therefore, Western hegemony has been a historical exception of only a couple of centuries, and now the pendulum of history is swinging back.

This means that if we are not the center of the world anymore, we also have to stop thinking as though we still were. Unfortunately, old prejudices, old assumptions, old attitudes, and old mentalities die hard. But in a new global environment, where the competition is between players coming from very different historical experiences and cultural backgrounds, it is fundamental to get out of our ethnocentric reference zone, shift our way of thinking, and develop a really global mindset. Those who are still stuck in a 20th century mentality cannot face the challenges of the 21st century.

Developing a global mindset means that while we remain rooted in our own cultural environment and our behaviour is shaped by our cultural values we are still able to "change gear" when dealing with people coming from other countries and cultures in order to be more effective in working, communicating and connecting with them. Truly global corporations have understood that. They have understood that, while strategies may be global, markets are local.

Within this global context in constant flux, China has become a central player that nobody can ignore. Even companies or business people that are not directly doing business in China are increasingly dealing with Chinese people, whether they are customers, investors, shareholders, managers or employees. The ability to develop a good understanding of China's cultural framework is therefore becoming very important, if not essential, for an increasing number of people around the world.

Developing cultural intelligence is not an easy process. It requires at first the ability to put one's own cultural references into a larger perspective and reach the awareness that what we do and the way we think and behave is subconsciously shaped by cultural values that we take for granted. Therefore, the way we think and behave is not universal, but related to a specific cultural framework. Other people from other cultures have other values that make them see the same thing in another way. Understanding their way of seeing things is therefore the first step towards gaining cultural intelligence.

Once we are able to see the reason behind other people's attitudes, once we identify the fault lines that divide different cultures, we will be capable of preventing misunderstandings and problems and create the right framework for more productive communication and cooperation. When it comes to China, this is definitely one of the keys to success. I hope that this book has given you at least a small key with which to open the door to a new horizon of new perspectives and opportunities.

[1] Livermore, David & Van Dyne, Linn, *Cultural Intelligence : The Essential Intelligence for the 21st Century*, SHRM Foundation, Alexandria, 2015, p. 2.

[2] Beugelsdijk, Sjoerd, Maseland, Robbert & Van Hoorn, André, « Are Scores on Hofstede's Dimensions of National Culture Stable Over Time ? A Cohort Analysis », in *Global Strategy Journal*, No. 5, p. 224, 2015.

9

九

REFERENCES

- Akgunes, Asuman & Culpepper, Robert, « Negotiations Between Chinese and Americans : Examining the Cultural Context and Salient Factors », in *The Journal of International Management Studies*, Vol. 7, No. 1, April 2012.
- Ascencio, Chloé & Rey, Dominique, *Travailler avec les Chinois. 8 clés opérationnelles pour réussir*, Dunod, Paris, 2016.
- Bains, Gurnek, *Cultural DNA. The psychology of globalization*, Wiley, Hoboken, 2015.
- Benoliel, Michael, « Negotiating Successfully in Asia », in *Eurasian Journal of Social Sciences*, 1(1), 2013.
- Beugelsdijk, Sjoerd, Maseland, Robbert & Van Hoorn, André, « Are Scores on Hofstede's Dimensions of National Culture Stable Over Time ?

A Cohort Analysis », in *Global Strategy Journal*, No. 5, 2015.

- Cai, Z., Morris, J. & Chen, J., « Explaining the human resource management preferences of employees : a study of China workers », in *The International Journal of Human Resource Management*, Vol. 22, Issue 16, 2011.

- Chen, Jie & Eldridge, Derek, « Are standardized performance appraisal practices really preferred ? A case study in China », in *Chinese Management Studies*, Vol. 4, No. 3, 2010.

- Chen, Li-Kai, Mourshed, Mona & Grant, Andrew, *The $250 billion question : Can China close the skills gap ?* , McKinsey & Company, May 2013.

- Cheng, Kevin H. C. & Cascio, Wayne, « Performance-Appraisal Beliefs of Chinese Employees in Hong Kong and the Pearl River Delta », in *International Journal of Selection and Assessment*, Vol. 17, No. 3, September 2009.

- Chmielecki, Michal, « HR Challenges in China », in *Journal of Intercultural Management*, Vol. 4, No. 3, September 2012.

- Chu, Chin-ning, *The Asian Mind Game. Unlocking the hidden agenda of the Asian business culture – A Westerner's survival manual*, Rawson Associates, New York, 1991.

- Doctoroff, Tom, *What Chinese Want. Culture, Communism, and China's Modern Consumer*, Palgrave Macmillan, New York, 2012.

- Fang, Tony, « Negotiation : the Chinese style », in *Journal of Business & Industrial Marketing*, 21/1, 2006.

- Fasching, Darrell J. & deChant, Dell, *Comparative Religious Ethics. A Narrative Approach to Global Ethics*, Wiley, Hoboken, 2001.

- Faure, Guy Olivier, « China : New Values in a Changing Society », *Euro China Forum*, http://www.ceibs.edu/ase/Documents/EuroChina Forum/faure.htm.

- Faure, Guy Olivier & Fang, Tony, « Changing Chinese values : Keeping up with paradoxes », in *International Business Review*, No. 17, 2008.

- Flisak, Daniel & Bjerkhage, Thomas, *How culture affects the motivation of employees. A study in differences in motivation between Swedish and Chinese employees*, Bachelor Thesis 15HP, University of Gothenburg, School of business, economics and law, June 2015.

- Fukuyama, Francis, *Trust : The Social Virtues and The Creation of Prosperity*, Free Press Paperbacks, New York, 1996.

- Gan, Shengfei, *How To Do Business With China. An Inside View on Chinese Culture and Etiquette*, Author House, Bloomington, 2014.

- Ghauri, Pervez & Fang, Tony, « Negotiating with the Chinese : A Socio-Cultural Analysis », in *Journal of World Business*, 36.3, Fall 2001.

- Hall, Edward T., *The Silent Language*, Anchor Books, New York, 1973.

- Hall, Edward T., *Beyond Culture*, Anchor Books, New York, 1989.

- Hofstede, Geert, Hofstede, Gert Jan & Minkov, Michael, *Cultures and Organizations. Software of the Mind*, McGraw Hill, New York, 2010.

- Javary, Cyrille J.-D., *La souplesse du dragon. Les fondamentaux de la culture chinoise*, Albin Michel, Paris, 2014.

- Ji, Li-Jun, Nisbett, Richard E. & Zhang, Zhiyong, « Is It Culture or Is It Language ? Examination of Language Effects in Cross-Cultural Research on Categorization », in *Journal of Personality and Social Psychology*, Vol. 87, No. 1, 2004.

- Jullien, François, *Traité de l'efficacité*, Grasset, Paris, 1996.
- KPMG Global China Practice, *China Outlook 2016*, KPMG, 2016.
- Kuo, Youchi, Walters, Jeff, Gao, Hongbing, Wang, Angela, Yang, Veronique, Yang, Jian, Lyu, Zhibin & Wan, Hongjie, *The New China Playbook. Young, Affluent, E-savvy Consumers Will Fuel Growth*, bcg perspectives, Boston Consulting Group, December 21, 2015.
- Lafayette De Mente, Boyé, *The Chinese Way In Business. The Secrets of Successful Business Dealings in China*, Tuttle Publishing, Tokyo-Rutland-Singapore, 2013.
- Lee, Kam-hon Lee, Yang, Guang & Graham, John L., "Tension and trust in international business negotiations: American executives negotiating with Chinese executives", in *Journal of International Business Studies*, 37, September 2006.
- « Les paradoxes de la gestion des RH », in *Connexions*, Hiver 2015-2016.
- Lewis, Richard D., *When Cultures Collide. Leading across cultures*, Nicholas Brealey International, Boston-London, 2006.
- Lewis, Richard, « How Different Cultures Understand Time », in *Business Insider*, 1.6.2014, http://www.businessinsider.com/how-different-cultures-understand-time-2014-5?IR=T.
- Li, Ma, « Epistemological Reasons for Lack of Science in Ancient China », in *Open Journal of Social Sciences*, 3, 2015.
- Livermore, David & Van Dyne, Linn, *Cultural Intelligence : The Essential Intelligence for the 21st Century*, SHRM Foundation, Alexandria, 2015.
- Manpower, « Winning in China : Building Talent Competitiveness », Manpower Inc., November 2010.

- March, Robert M. & Wu, Su-Hua, *The Chinese Negotiator. How to Succeed in the World's Largest Market*, Kodansha International, Tokyo-New York-London, 2007.
- Michael Page, *2016 Greater China Employee Intentions Report*, Michael Page, October 2015.
- Mooij de, Marieke and Hofstede, Geert, « Cross-Cultural Consumer Behavior : A Review of Research Findings », in *Journal of International Consumer Marketing*, 23 :p. 183, 2011.
- Nie, Winter, « Talent management in China : It is not one-size-fits-all », *Swiss Re Centre for Global Dialogue*, 26.5.2015, http://cgd.swissre.com/risk_dialogue_magazine/Talent_in_China/Talent_management_in_China_It_is_not_one-size-fits-all.html.
- Nisbett, Richard E. et al., « Culture and Systems of Thought : Holistic Versus Analytic Cognition », in *Psychological Review*, Vol. 108, No. 2, 2001.
- Nisbett, Richard E. & Miyamoto, Yuri, « The influence of culture : holistic versus analytic perception », in *Trends in Cognitive Sciences*, Vol. 9, No. 10, October 2005.
- Nisbett, Richard E., *The Geography of Thought. How Asians and Westerners Think Differently...and Why*, Nicholas Brealey Publishing, London-Boston, 2010.
- Raynaud, Christine & Eagan, Angie, « Company Culture in Building a Strong and Stable Workforce in China », *China Business Review*, 8.11.2013.
- Roth, Hans J., « Personnel Management in China », *Swiss Re Centre for Global Dialogue*, 26.5.2015, http://cgd.swissre.com/risk_dialogue_magazine/Talent_in_China/Personnel_Management_in_China.html.

- Schell, Orville & Delury, John, *Wealth and Power. China's long march to the Twenty-First Century*, Random House, New York, 2013.
- Schuman, Michael, *Confucius And the World He Created*, Basic Books, New York, 2015.
- Sebenius, James K. & Qiang, Cheng, « Cultural Notes on Chinese Negotiating Behavior », *Harvard Business School*, Working Paper 09-076, December 24, 2008.
- Shuang, Liu & Chen, Guo-Ming, « Assessing Chinese Conflict Management Styles in Joint Ventures », in *Intercultural Communication Studies*, IX-2, 2000.
- Turner, Stephen P., *How to Win in China. Business and Negotiation Strategies Revealed*, L&T Publishing, Austin, 2011.
- Vahle, Gina R., Bursen, Tony, *Managing in China. The Truth about Cultural Differences in the Chinese Workplace*, Expat Guide, 2014.
- Veldohen, Steven, Peng, Bill, Mansson, Anna, Yip, George & Han, Jian, *China's innovation is going global. 2014 China innovation survey*, Strategy&, 2015.
- Wang, Jia, Wang, Greg G., Ruona, Wendy E. A. & Rojewski, Jay W., « Confucian Values and the Implications for International HRD », in *Human Resource Development International*, Vol. 8, No. 3, September 2005.
- Wee, Chow-Hou & Combe, Fred, *Business Journey to the East. An East-West Perspective on Global-is-Asian*, McGraw-Hill, Singapore, 2009.
- Wee, Chow-Hou, « An Integrative Perspective on *Guanxi* : Dispelling Myths to Facilitate Business in China », in *Global Business and Organizational Excellence*, Vol. 34, Issue 1, November/December 2014.
- Wei, Xiaohong & Li, Qingyuan, « The Confucian Value of Harmony and its Influence on Chinese

Social Interaction », in *Cross-Cultural Communication*, Vol. 9, No. 1, 2013.

- Xu, Xiuyan, « Cultural Factors in EAP Teaching – Influences of Thought Pattern on English Academic Writing », in *Cross-cultural communication*, Vol. 8, No. 4, 2012.
- Yang, Fang, « The Importance of Guanxi to Multinational Companies in China », in *Asian Social Science*, Vol. 7, No. 7, July 2011.
- Yang, Fang, « Work, motivation and personal characteristics : an in-depth study of six organizations in Ningbo », in *Chinese Management Studies*, Vol. 5, No. 3, 2011.
- Yin, Fei, « An Analysis on Factors of Success for Chinese/European JVs in Culture Aspect », in *International Journal of Business and Management*, Vol. 3, No. 6, June 2008.
- Zeng, Rong & Greenfield, Patricia M., « Cultural evolution over the last 40 years in China : Using the Google Ngram Viewer to study implications of social and political change for cultural values », in *International Journal of Psychology*, Vol. 50, No. 1, 2015.
- Zhang, Weiwei, *The China Wave. Rise of a Civilizational State*, World Century, Hackensack, 2012.
- Zhang, Haihua & Baker, Geoff, *Think Like Chinese*, The Federation Press, Annandale, 2013.
- Zhu, Jiang & Bao, Yuxiao, « The Pragmatic Comparison of Chinese and Western Politeness in Cross-cultural Communication », in *Journal of Language Teaching and Research*, Vol. 1, No. 6, November 2010